Women Abolitionist and Their Impact on Liberation

By Lois Denise Africa

Dedicated to the

""I will be heard"

In many locations they could not vote nor own property. They were sometimes used like chattel to secure advantages in business deals and were often pawns in marriage discussions. Overall, they had no legal right to even decide the education, religion or the residence of their own children

If this sounds like slavery to you, then a rose by any other name may in some instances be what it was, for women in America. With the exception of the widespread murder, kidnapping and other crimes that African Americans were saddled with, there were stark similarities. In this instance however, it pertains to the plight of women in some locations during the early years of the United States. Many of these same heroines to which this book is dedicated., that excercised extraordinary efforts to bring down slavery, were not technically "free" themselves. The Emancipation Proclamation did nothing to improve their lot or remove the archaic laws and customs that prevailed at the time. So while others were being proclaimed free and laws were changing, (largely through their efforts,) they remained relatively "Unemancipated." Tough to imagine, but the following segment from the Seneca Falls Declaration of 1848, delivered by Elizabeth Cady Stanton sums it up.(full copy at conclusion of the book).

"Now, in view of this entire disfranchisement of one-half the people of this country, their social and religious degradation, in view of the unjust laws above mentioned, and because women do feel themselves aggrieved, oppressed, and fraudulently deprived of their most sacred rights, we insist that they have immediate admission to all the rights and privileges which belong to them as citizens of the United States."

So, for these remarkable women, the abolition of slavery was only the appetizer; and not the main course. The Juneteenth like events were just a steppingstone to our becoming "that" nation that "held these truths to be self-evident that all MEN AND WOMEN were created equal. A concept that was in line with the "Give me Liberty or Give me Death" theme of the Revolutionary War and the "Ride or Die" one of the present.

Case in point is that from shortly after the wars end and going forward until Jim Crow and Black Laws became robust enough to completely smother the intended emancipation gains, women in many communities had even fewer legislated rights than Black or African

Sadly, access to the most important freedom, the right to vote did not arrive until the 19th Amendment to the United States constitution, as ratified on August 18, 1920, arrived. As follows:

"Section 1: The right of citizens of the United States to vote shall not be denied or abridged by the United States or by any State on account of sex.

Section 2: Congress shall have power to enforce this article by appropriate legislation."

Yet many American women fought tirelessly to win freedom for those that had been most marginalized and enslaved.

So, to these **"Founding Mothers"** of the true America Liberty, I dedicate this book, while thanking them deeply for doing God's work when others looked the other way. I thank them for not ignoring the cry of their sister, Sojourner Truth, who spoke to their pain as well.

"Ain't I a woman?

Look at me! Look at my arm! I have ploughed and planted, and gathered into barns, and no man could head me!

And ain't I a woman?

I could work as much and eat as much as a man - when I could get it - and bear the lash as well!

And ain't I a woman?

I have borne thirteen children, and seen most all sold off to slavery, and when I cried out with my mother's grief, none but Jesus heard me!

And ain't I a woman?" –

Contents

Introduction 3

Famous Quotes by Female Abolitionists 6

Sarah and Angelina Grimké - Sisters of Liberation 9

Lucretia Mott - Voice of Equality 12

Elizabeth Cady Stanton- Co-authored the Declaration of Sentiments 14

Lucy Stone- Co-founder of the American Anti-Slavery Society/Co-founder of the American Woman Suffrage Association 16

Susan B. Anthony - Founder of the Women's Loyal National League 18

Sarah Parker Remond - A Voice for Freedom 20

Lydia Maria Child - A Pen for Justice 22

Harriet Beecher Stowe - Author of Uncle Tom's Cabin 24

Abby Kelley Foster - A Voice for Equality 26

Amelia Bloomer - "The Lily," one of the first newspapers for women 28

Julia Ward Howe - Author of "The Battle Hymn of the Republic" 30

Antoinette Brown Blackwell - First woman to be ordained as a minister in the United States 32

Maria Weston Chapman - Editor of "The Liberty Bell 34

Sarah Josepha Hale - Editor of the "Ladies' Magazine 36

Mary Livermore - A Trailblazer for Equality and Justice 39

Susan Paul - A Voice for Freedom 41

Ellen Craft - A Brave Journey to Freedom 43

Emily Howland - Pioneer in Abolitionism and Women's Rights 45

Hannah More - A Beacon of Enlightenment and Compassion 48

Anne Knight – British Voice for Equality and Truth 51

Elizabeth Heyrick A Tireless Advocate for Immediate Emancipation 54

Mary Prince The Voice of Resistance and Resilience 57

Mary Ann McCracken - A Champion for Justice in Ireland 59

Jane Grey Swisshelm - A Pen of Conviction and Courage 62

Matilda Joslyn Gage - A Crusader for Women's Rights and Abolition 65

Martha Coffin Wright -Hope on the Underground Railroad 68

Rebecca Buffum Spring - Eloquent and Passionate 70

Catharine Beecher - A Pioneer of Education and Social Reform 72

Frances Wright - A Trailblazer for Social Reform 75

Mary White Ovington - Co-founder of the NAACP 78

Caroline Weston - Keen intellect and a thirst for knowledge 81

Dorothea Dix - Social Reform and Humanitarian Champion 84

Mary Townsend Seymour -Trailblazer for Suffrage and Civil Rights 88

Clara Barton - Founder of the Red Cross 91

Lydia White Shattuck - A Champion for Justice and Equality 94

Anna Elizabeth Dickinson – Impassioned Voice of Emancipation 97

Sarah Margaret Fuller - A Voice for Social Reform/Women's Rights 100

Lillie Devereux Blake - A Trailblazer for Women's Rights 103

Harriet Tubman - Underground Railroad Conductor/Union Soldier 106

Conclusion 109

When and where women gained the right to vote 111

The Seneca Falls Declaration 1848 115

Birthdates 121

Introduction

The Vital Role of Women Abolitionists to the Reality of Emancipation

Juneteenth, celebrated annually on June 19th, commemorates the emancipation of enslaved African Americans in the United States. While the Emancipation Proclamation of 1863 marked a significant step toward ending slavery, it was not until June 19, 1865, that Union soldiers arrived in Galveston, Texas, bringing news of freedom to the last enslaved individuals.

Behind this pivotal moment in history lies a tapestry of abolitionist efforts, with women playing a crucial role. This book explores the importance of women abolitionists in the reality of Juneteenth, highlighting their legislation, activism, actions, movements, and other contributions that led to the abolition of slavery.

Legislation and Policy Reform

Women abolitionists played a vital role in advocating for legislative and policy reforms that ultimately contributed to the end of slavery. One notable figure is Harriet Beecher Stowe, whose novel "Uncle Tom's Cabin" (1852) ignited public outrage against the institution of slavery. Stowe's vivid portrayal of the brutal realities faced by enslaved individuals humanized the abolitionist cause and contributed to the growing anti-slavery sentiment across the nation.

Similarly, Angelina Grimké and her sister Sarah Grimké were prominent abolitionists who utilized their platform to advocate for legislative change. They authored pamphlets, delivered speeches, and lobbied lawmakers to enact laws that would abolish slavery. Their efforts helped to shape public opinion and galvanize support for the abolitionist movement.

Activism and Grassroots Organizing

Women abolitionists were at the forefront of grassroots organizing and activism, mobilizing communities and fostering networks of resistance against slavery. Sojourner Truth, an African American abolitionist and women's rights activist, traveled across the country delivering powerful speeches that exposed the injustices of slavery and advocated for its abolition. Truth's famous "Ain't I a Woman?" speech delivered at the

Women's Rights Convention in Akron, Ohio, in 1851, highlighted the intersectionality of race and gender in the fight for equality.

Additionally, Lydia Maria Child, a prolific writer and abolitionist, used her pen to advocate for social reform and challenge the institution of slavery. Her writings, including "An Appeal in Favor of That Class of Americans Called Africans" (1833), provided a moral and intellectual framework for the abolitionist movement, inspiring countless individuals to join the cause.

Actions and Underground Railroad

Women abolitionists played a crucial role in the operation of the Underground Railroad, a clandestine network of safe houses and routes used to aid enslaved individuals escaping to freedom. Harriet Tubman, often referred to as the "Moses of her people," was a fearless conductor on the Underground Railroad, leading hundreds of enslaved individuals to freedom in the North.

Similarly, Martha Coffin Wright, a Quaker abolitionist, and women's rights activist, worked alongside Tubman and other abolitionists to provide shelter, food, and support to freedom seekers. Wright's involvement in the Underground Railroad exemplifies the vital role that women played in facilitating the escape of enslaved individuals and undermining the institution of slavery from within.

Movements and Organizations

Women abolitionists were instrumental in the formation of abolitionist movements and organizations that advocated for the immediate abolition of slavery. The American Anti-Slavery Society, founded in 1833 by prominent abolitionists including Angelina Grimké and Sarah Grimké, was one such organization that played a central role in galvanizing public opposition to slavery.

Similarly, the National Women's Anti-Slavery Convention, organized by Lucretia Mott and Elizabeth Cady Stanton in 1837, brought together women abolitionists from across the country to strategize and coordinate their efforts. The convention provided a platform for women to amplify their voices and assert their leadership within the abolitionist movement.

Contributions to Emancipation

The contributions of women abolitionists to the abolition of slavery cannot be overstated. While the Emancipation Proclamation of 1863 marked a significant milestone in the fight against slavery, it was the persistent advocacy and activism of women abolitionists that paved the way for its eventual implementation.

Women like Frances Ellen Watkins Harper, an African American abolitionist and suffragist, continued to advocate for the rights of formerly enslaved individuals following emancipation. Harper's work as a lecturer and writer helped to shape public discourse on issues of racial justice and equality in the post-emancipation era.

Conclusion

In conclusion, women abolitionists played a vital role in the emergence of Juneteenth and the ultimate abolition of slavery in the United States. Through their legislation, activism, actions, movements, and other contributions, women abolitionists helped to galvanize public opposition to slavery, mobilize communities, and pave the way for legislative and policy reforms that ultimately led to emancipation. As we commemorate Juneteenth and celebrate the achievements of the abolitionist movement, let us remember the invaluable contributions of women abolitionists who fought tirelessly for freedom, justice, and equality for all.

Famous Quotes by Female Abolitionists

"The cause of freedom is not the cause of a race or a sect, a party or a class—it is the cause of humankind." - Mary Livermore

"Right is of no sex - truth is of no color - God is the Father of us all, and we are all brethren." - Susan Paul

"Now all we need is to continue to speak the truth fearlessly, and we shall add to our number those who will turn the scale to the side of equal and full justice in all things." - Lucy Stone

"I ask no favors for my sex. I surrender not our claim to equality. All I ask of our brethren is that they take their feet from off our necks and permit us to stand upright on the ground which God has designed us to occupy." - Sarah Moore Grimké

"Organize, agitate, educate, must be our war cry." - Susan B. Anthony

"To say that any people are not fit for freedom is to make poverty their choice." - Sarah Josepha Hale

"In a world where there is so much to be done, I felt strongly impressed that there must be something for me to do." - Dorothea Dix

"I want to be identified with the negro; until he gets his rights, we shall never have ours." - Sarah Parker Remond

"The remedy for wrongs is to forget them." - Lydia Maria Child

"The bitterest tears shed over graves are for words left unsaid and deeds left undone." - Harriet Beecher Stowe

"We cannot be just to others without being just to ourselves." - Abby Kelley Foster

"We will be the sufferers if you make us shut out from the sun, water, and air. These things are the best elements of life." - Amelia Bloomer

"I feel that the influence of woman will save the country before every other power." - Julia Ward Howe

"I appeal to women, by their hopes and their aspirations, to aid us in lifting the standard of freedom." - Angelina Grimké Weld

"Let no one seek his own, but each one another's wealth." - Caroline Weston

"We have won the battle when we believe we can." - Antoinette Brown Blackwell

"Slavery is not abolished until the black man has the ballot." - Maria Weston Chapman

"Let us consecrate ourselves to the service of humanity." - Sarah Josepha Hale

"The fight must be bitter and hard against the enormous prejudices of society." - Mary Livermore

"I have always contended that our God is a God of love.

"The slave has but one master, the abolitionist has none." - Sarah Grimké

"Injustice anywhere is a threat to justice everywhere." - Lucretia Mott

"The best protection any woman can have is courage." - Elizabeth Cady Stanton

"Now all we need is to continue to speak the truth fearlessly, and we shall add to our number those who will turn the scale to the side of equal and full justice in all things." - Lucy Stone

"It is your duty to tell us, not about some future existence, but about this life, about injustice." - Sarah Parker Remond

"The past, the present, and the future are really one: they are today." - Harriet Beecher Stowe

"No one is free until all are free." - Abby Kelley Foster

"We should not permit our grievances to overshadow our opportunities." - Amelia Bloomer

"The sword of murder is not the balance of justice." - Julia Ward Howe

"If slavery is not wrong, nothing is wrong." - Angelina Grimké Weld

One's work may be finished some day, but one's education never." - Caroline Weston

"In a world where there is so much to be done, I felt strongly impressed that there must be something for me to do." - Dorothea Dix

"Truth makes men free." - Antoinette Brown Blackwell

"We must unite in solemn and earnest efforts to crush the monster." - Maria Weston Chapman

"In the condition of the slave, the two sexes have been uniformly degraded, equally subjected to the lash of brutal task-masters." - Sarah Moore Grimké

"The United States government must demand for all, and protect the rights of all, its citizens." - Abby Kelley Foster

"Slavery is a foul sin against God and man." - Angelina Grimké Weld

"Truth is powerful and it prevails." - Sojourner Truth

"The only way to right wrongs is to turn the light of truth upon them." - Ida B. Wells

"The abolition of slavery must be in pursuance of some great principles, and to follow up this principle, the leaders in this movement must teach others to obey, not men, but God." - Harriet Beecher Stowe

"I would fight for my liberty so long as my strength lasted." - Harriet Tubman

"The doctrine of slavery is no longer a question for discussion; it is settled, thank God, for the earth's remaining years." - Maria Weston Chapman

"There is no slave, after all, like a wife." - Elizabeth Cady Stanton

"God made me to do the best that I can, and I have done it." - Sojourner Truth

"I freed a thousand slaves. I could have freed a thousand more if only they knew they were slaves." - Harriet Tubman

"Every moment's experience on the side of slavery is a moment's experience against it." - Harriet Martineau

"The true republic: men, their rights, and nothing more; women, their rights, and nothing less." - Susan B. Anthony

Sarah and Angelina Grimké

Sisters of Liberation

In the heart of Charleston, South Carolina, in the late 18th century, two sisters were born into a world of privilege and contradiction. Sarah Moore Grimké, the eldest, entered the world in 1792, followed by her sister Angelina Emily Grimké in 1805. Their father, Judge John Grimké, was a prominent figure in the community, serving as a judge and a member of the state legislature. Their mother, Mary Smith Grimké, hailed from a wealthy plantation-owning family, adding to the Grimké sisters' upbringing of luxury and privilege.

From a young age, Sarah and Angelina were acutely aware of the stark disparities of their world. The Grimké household, like many others in the South, relied on the labor of enslaved people to maintain its opulence. However, unlike their peers, Sarah and Angelina harbored a deep sense of unease and moral conflict about the institution of slavery.

As the sisters grew older, they began to question the status quo more openly. Sarah, the more introspective and scholarly of the two, delved into literature and philosophy, seeking answers to the ethical dilemmas that plagued her. Angelina, fiery and passionate, chafed against the constraints placed upon women in society, yearning for a platform from which to advocate for change.

Despite their differences, Sarah and Angelina shared a bond forged in their shared convictions. Together, they embarked on a journey of self-discovery and activism that would ultimately reshape the course of American history.

In 1819, Sarah married Theodore Dwight Weld, a fervent abolitionist and minister. Weld shared Sarah's ardor for justice and equality, and the two formed a formidable partnership in the fight against slavery. Meanwhile, Angelina, still unmarried, found herself increasingly drawn to the abolitionist cause, inspired by the impassioned speeches of William Lloyd Garrison and the writings of Frederick Douglass.

In 1830, the Grimké sisters made a momentous decision that would alter the course of their lives forever. They left behind their comfortable existence in Charleston and moved to Philadelphia, a hotbed of abolitionist activity. There, they became deeply involved in the burgeoning abolitionist movement, attending meetings, organizing rallies, and speaking out against the evils of slavery.

Their newfound activism did not come without consequences, however. Back in Charleston, their family disowned them, casting them out as pariahs for daring to challenge the institution of slavery. Undeterred, Sarah and Angelina pressed on, their resolve only strengthened by the persecution they faced.

As the years passed, the Grimké sisters' influence within the abolitionist movement continued to grow. In 1836, they published "American Slavery As It Is: Testimony of a Thousand Witnesses," a groundbreaking indictment of the horrors of slavery based on firsthand accounts from enslaved individuals themselves. The book sent shockwaves through the nation, exposing the brutal reality of slavery to a wider audience than ever before.

But Sarah and Angelina's activism was not limited to the abolitionist cause alone. Inspired by their own experiences of oppression as women, they also became vocal advocates for women's rights. In 1838, Angelina delivered her famous "Appeal to the Christian Women of the South," urging women to rise up against the injustices perpetrated against them and to claim their rightful place in society.

In 1840, Sarah and Angelina made history as the first women to address a legislative body in the United States. They testified before the Massachusetts State Legislature, advocating for the abolition of slavery and the enfranchisement of women. Though their efforts were met with resistance and hostility, they refused to be silenced, determined to speak truth to power no matter the cost.

As the years wore on, the Grimké sisters continued to be trailblazers in the fight for justice and equality. They traveled the country, speaking to packed auditoriums and inspiring countless others to join the cause. Despite facing threats to their safety and relentless criticism from their detractors, they remained steadfast in their commitment to their principles.

In their later years, Sarah and Angelina witnessed the fruits of their labor as the abolitionist movement gained momentum and the tide of public opinion began to turn against slavery. Though they did not live to see the abolition of slavery themselves, they knew that their efforts had laid the groundwork for future generations to carry on the fight.

Sarah passed away in 1873, followed by Angelina in 1879. Though they may have departed this world, their legacy lived on, a testament to the power of courage, conviction, and sisterhood in the pursuit of justice.

Today, the Grimké sisters are remembered as pioneers of the abolitionist and women's rights movements, their names forever etched in the annals of history as symbols of courage and resilience in the face of oppression. Their story serves as a reminder that ordinary individuals have the power to effect extraordinary change, and that the fight for justice is a journey that knows no bounds.

Lucretia Mott

Voice of Equality

https://nha.org/wp-content/uploads/Lucretia-Mott-Portrait-Swarthmore.jpg

In the quiet countryside of Nantucket, Massachusetts, on January 3, 1793, Lucretia Coffin entered the world, destined to become one of the most influential voices for justice and equality in American history. Born into a devout Quaker family, Lucretia was instilled with the values of compassion, empathy, and social justice from an early age.

Lucretia's childhood was marked by a deep sense of moral responsibility and a fierce commitment to her Quaker faith. Raised in a community that valued simplicity, equality, and nonviolence, she was taught to see the inherent worth and dignity of every human being, regardless of race, gender, or social status.

At the tender age of thirteen, Lucretia met James Mott, a fellow Quaker and abolitionist, who would become her lifelong partner and ally in the fight for justice. The two were married in 1811, and together they embarked on a journey of shared purpose and mutual respect that would span nearly seven decades.

From the outset, Lucretia and James Mott's marriage was characterized by a deep commitment to equality and social reform. They shared a common vision of a world free from oppression and injustice, and they worked tirelessly together to bring that vision to fruition.

In 1818, Lucretia gave birth to her first child, a daughter named Maria. Motherhood only strengthened Lucretia's resolve to create a better world for future generations, and she threw herself wholeheartedly into the struggle for social justice.

As Lucretia's activism grew, so too did the backlash from those who sought to maintain the status quo. The Mott family faced persecution and ostracism from their community, as their outspoken advocacy for abolition and women's rights drew the ire of their more conservative peers.

Undeterred by the threats and intimidation, Lucretia continued to speak out against injustice with unwavering courage and conviction. She traveled the country, delivering impassioned speeches and sermons on the evils of slavery and the importance of women's equality.

In 1840, Lucretia played a pivotal role in the founding of the American Anti-Slavery Society, alongside her friend and fellow abolitionist William Lloyd Garrison. Together, they worked tirelessly to mobilize public opinion against the institution of slavery, organizing rallies, circulating petitions, and distributing anti-slavery literature.

But Lucretia's activism was not limited to the abolitionist cause alone. In 1848, she helped organize the historic Seneca Falls Convention, the first women's rights convention in American history. There, she delivered a stirring address calling for women's suffrage and equal rights under the law, laying the groundwork for the modern women's rights movement.

Throughout her life, Lucretia remained steadfast in her commitment to justice and equality, even as she faced criticism and condemnation from those who sought to silence her. She continued to advocate for the rights of the marginalized and oppressed until her dying breath, leaving behind a legacy that continues to inspire generations of activists to this day.

Lucretia Mott passed away on November 11, 1880, but her spirit lives on in the countless individuals whose lives have been touched by her courage, her compassion, and her unwavering dedication to the cause of justice. Today, she is remembered as a trailblazer, a visionary, and a tireless champion of equality for all.

Elizabeth Cady Stanton

Architect of Equality

Co-authored the Declaration of Sentiments

Elizabeth Cady Stanton (1815-1902): Stanton was a leader in the women's suffrage movement but was also active in the abolitionist cause. She advocated for the rights of both women and African Americans.

On November 12, 1815, in the bustling town of Johnstown, New York, Elizabeth Cady was born into a world on the cusp of transformation. Raised in a household steeped in privilege and tradition, Elizabeth's early years were marked by a keen intellect and an insatiable curiosity about the world around her.

Elizabeth's upbringing was shaped by her father, Daniel Cady, a prominent attorney and judge, who encouraged her to pursue her education and develop her intellect. Despite the limitations placed upon women in the early 19th century, Elizabeth's parents instilled in her a belief in her own worth and a determination to defy the constraints of society.

In 1840, Elizabeth married Henry Brewster Stanton, a prominent abolitionist and reformer, with whom she shared a deep commitment to social justice. Together, they embarked on a partnership that would prove to be both transformative and tumultuous, as they navigated the complexities of marriage and activism in a society that was hostile to both.

As Elizabeth's activism grew, so too did the backlash from those who sought to maintain the status quo. She faced ridicule and condemnation from her peers, who viewed her advocacy for women's rights as radical and subversive. Undeterred by the criticism, Elizabeth continued to speak out against injustice with unwavering courage and conviction.

In 1848, Elizabeth played a pivotal role in organizing the historic Seneca Falls Convention, the first women's rights convention in American history. There, she delivered a stirring address calling for women's suffrage and equal rights under the law, laying the groundwork for the modern women's rights movement.

But Elizabeth's activism was not limited to the women's suffrage movement alone. She was also a vocal advocate for the abolition of slavery, working alongside her husband and other abolitionists to mobilize public opinion against the institution of slavery. Together, they attended anti-slavery meetings, circulated petitions, and authored articles for abolitionist newspapers.

As the years passed, Elizabeth's commitment to social justice only grew stronger. She co-authored the Declaration of Sentiments, a groundbreaking document that called for an end to the legal and social inequalities faced by women, and she continued to speak out against discrimination and oppression in all its forms.

Despite facing persecution and opposition at every turn, Elizabeth never wavered in her belief that all people were entitled to equality and justice. She continued to fight for the rights of women and African Americans until her dying breath, leaving behind a legacy that continues to inspire generations of activists to this day.

Elizabeth Cady Stanton passed away on October 26, 1902, but her spirit lives on in the countless individuals whose lives have been touched by her courage, her compassion, and her unwavering dedication to the cause of justice. Today, she is remembered as a trailblazer, a visionary, and a tireless champion of equality for all.

Lucy Stone

A Voice for Justice

Lucy Stone (1818-1893): Stone was a prominent abolitionist and suffragist. She co-founded the American Anti-Slavery Society and the American Woman Suffrage Association.

Lucy Stone came into the world on August 13, 1818, in West Brookfield, Massachusetts, a time when the United States was grappling with issues of slavery and women's rights. Born to Francis Stone and Hannah Matthews, Lucy was raised in a family that valued education and social justice. Her parents instilled in her a strong sense of morality and a belief in the inherent dignity of all people, regardless of race or gender.

As a young girl, Lucy exhibited a sharp intellect and a fierce independence that would define her life's work. Despite the limited educational opportunities available to women at the time, Lucy was determined to pursue her studies. She attended local schools and later enrolled at Mount Holyoke Female Seminary, where she distinguished herself as a talented student.

In 1843, Lucy graduated from Oberlin College, becoming one of the first women in the United States to earn a college degree. It was during her time at Oberlin that Lucy became involved in the abolitionist movement, attending anti-slavery meetings and lectures and joining the ranks of those who were working to bring an end to the institution of slavery.

In 1850, Lucy married Henry Browne Blackwell, a prominent abolitionist and women's rights activist. Their marriage was unconventional for the time, as they both retained their own names and refused to include the word "obey" in their wedding vows. Together, they embarked on a partnership based on mutual respect and shared values, working side by side in the fight for justice and equality.

As Lucy's activism grew, so too did the backlash from those who sought to maintain the status quo. She faced criticism and condemnation from her peers, who viewed her advocacy for women's rights as radical and subversive. Undeterred by the opposition, Lucy continued to speak out against injustice with unwavering courage and conviction.

In 1869, Lucy co-founded the American Woman Suffrage Association (AWSA), a pioneering organization dedicated to securing the right to vote for women. She served as the organization's first president, leading the charge for women's suffrage and equal rights under the law.

Throughout her life, Lucy remained committed to the principles of justice and equality, advocating for the rights of women and marginalized communities until her dying breath. She continued to inspire generations of activists with her courage, her compassion, and her unwavering dedication to the cause of justice.

Lucy Stone passed away on October 18, 1893, but her legacy lives on in the countless individuals whose lives have been touched by her tireless advocacy and her unwavering commitment to equality for all. Today, she is remembered as a trailblazer, a visionary, and a true pioneer in the fight for women's rights.

Susan B. Anthony

Trailblazer for Equality

Wherever women gather together failure is impossible

Susan B. Anthony (1820-1906): Anthony was a leading figure in the women's suffrage movement, but she was also active in the abolitionist cause. She campaigned tirelessly for both causes throughout her life.

Susan Brownell Anthony was born on February 15, 1820, in Adams, Massachusetts, into a family deeply committed to social justice and equality. Her parents, Daniel Anthony and Lucy Read, were Quakers who believed in the principles of simplicity, pacifism, and equality for all.

From a young age, Susan was imbued with a sense of moral responsibility and a belief in the inherent worth and dignity of every individual. Raised in a household that valued education and social activism, she was encouraged to think critically and to question the status quo.

As a young woman, Susan's passion for social justice only grew stronger. She became involved in the temperance movement, advocating for the abolition of alcohol consumption, which she saw as a scourge on society. It was during her involvement in the temperance movement that Susan first became acquainted with the interconnected issues of women's rights and abolition.

In 1851, Susan met Elizabeth Cady Stanton, a fellow activist and suffragist, at an anti-slavery conference in Seneca Falls, New York. The two women formed a lifelong partnership that would change the course of history. Together, they worked tirelessly to advance the cause of women's suffrage and equal rights under the law.

In 1854, Susan embarked on a speaking tour of New York State, delivering impassioned speeches on the need for women's suffrage and equal rights. Her eloquence and conviction captivated audiences across the state, earning her a reputation as one of the most dynamic and influential speakers of her time.

Despite facing ridicule and condemnation from those who opposed her radical ideas, Susan remained undaunted in her quest for justice and equality. She continued to travel the country, speaking out against injustice and advocating for the rights of women and marginalized communities.

In 1863, Susan founded the Women's Loyal National League, a pioneering organization dedicated to securing the abolition of slavery. She tirelessly lobbied Congress to pass the Thirteenth Amendment, which abolished slavery in the United States, and she personally collected thousands of signatures in support of the amendment.

But Susan's activism was not limited to the abolitionist cause alone. She also played a key role in the women's suffrage movement, tirelessly advocating for women's right to vote. In 1869, she founded the National Woman Suffrage Association (NWSA) alongside Elizabeth Cady Stanton, serving as its first president.

Throughout her life, Susan faced persecution and opposition from those who sought to maintain the status quo. She was arrested and fined for attempting to vote in the 1872 presidential election, an act of civil disobedience that brought national attention to the cause of women's suffrage.

Despite the setbacks and challenges she faced, Susan remained steadfast in her commitment to justice and equality. She continued to work tirelessly for the rights of women and marginalized communities until her dying breath.

Susan B. Anthony passed away on March 13, 1906, but her legacy lives on in the countless individuals whose lives have been touched by her courage, her conviction, and her unwavering dedication to the cause of justice. Today, she is remembered as a trailblazer, a visionary, and a true pioneer in the fight for women's rights.

Sarah Parker Remond

A Voice for Freedom

Sarah Parker Remond (1826-1894): Remond was an African American abolitionist and lecturer. She traveled extensively in both the United States and Europe, advocating for the abolition of slavery.

Sarah Parker Remond was born on June 6, 1826, in Salem, Massachusetts, into a family of prominent abolitionists and activists. Her parents, John and Nancy Remond, were both active in the anti-slavery movement, and they instilled in Sarah a deep sense of justice and a passion for social reform from a young age.

Growing up in Salem, Sarah was surrounded by a community of like-minded individuals who were dedicated to fighting against the evils of slavery. She attended integrated schools and was exposed to the harsh realities of racism and discrimination from an early age. Despite the challenges she faced, Sarah was determined to make a difference in the world.

In 1843, at the age of seventeen, Sarah embarked on her first speaking tour, delivering impassioned speeches on the need for the abolition of slavery. Her eloquence and conviction captivated audiences across the country, earning her a reputation as a powerful and dynamic speaker.

Throughout the 1840s and 1850s, Sarah continued to travel extensively, speaking out against slavery and advocating for the rights of African Americans. She traveled throughout the United States, from New England to the Deep South, spreading her message of freedom and equality wherever she went.

In 1856, Sarah embarked on a tour of Europe, where she became an international sensation. She delivered lectures in England, Scotland, and Ireland, captivating audiences with her eloquence and passion. She also met with prominent abolitionists and activists, including Frederick Douglass and William Lloyd Garrison, who helped to amplify her message on both sides of the Atlantic.

Despite her successes, Sarah faced persecution and opposition from those who sought to silence her. She was subjected to threats and harassment, and she often had to travel under the protection of armed guards. But Sarah refused to be intimidated, and she continued to speak out against injustice with unwavering courage and conviction.

In addition to her work as an abolitionist, Sarah was also a vocal advocate for women's rights. She believed strongly in the need for women to have a voice in society and fought tirelessly for their right to vote and participate in the political process.

In 1865, Sarah returned to the United States, where she continued to be a leading voice in the abolitionist movement. She joined the newly-formed American Equal Rights Association, which fought for both women's suffrage and African American civil rights. She also became involved in the women's suffrage movement, working alongside Susan B. Anthony and Elizabeth Cady Stanton to secure the right to vote for women.

Throughout her life, Sarah Parker Remond remained steadfast in her commitment to justice and equality. She continued to fight for the rights of African Americans and women until her dying breath, leaving behind a legacy that continues to inspire generations of activists to this day.

Sarah passed away on December 13, 1894, but her spirit lives on in the countless individuals whose lives have been touched by her courage, her conviction, and her unwavering dedication to the cause of freedom and equality. Today, she is remembered as a trailblazer, a visionary, and a true pioneer in the fight for social justice.

Lydia Maria Child

A Pen for Justice

Lydia Maria Child (1802-1880): Child was a prolific writer and abolitionist. She wrote extensively on the subject of slavery and was active in various abolitionist organizations.

Lydia Maria Child was born on February 11, 1802, in Medford, Massachusetts, into a family of modest means. Her parents, David and Susannah Francis, instilled in her a love of learning and a deep sense of compassion from a young age. Despite their limited resources, they encouraged Lydia to pursue her education and to use her talents to make a difference in the world.

From an early age, Lydia showed a remarkable aptitude for writing, penning poems and stories that captured the hearts of those around her. Encouraged by her parents, she continued to hone her craft, eventually publishing her first book, "Hobomok: A Tale of Early Times," in 1824.

In 1828, Lydia married David Lee Child, a lawyer and abolitionist, who shared her passion for social justice. Their marriage was marked by mutual respect and admiration, and they worked together to advance the cause of abolition and women's rights throughout their lives.

As Lydia's writing career flourished, so too did her activism. In 1833, she published "An Appeal in Favor of That Class of Americans Called Africans," a groundbreaking work that called for the immediate abolition of slavery. The book was met with widespread acclaim and helped to galvanize public opinion against the institution of slavery.

Throughout the 1830s and 1840s, Lydia continued to write extensively on the subject of slavery, publishing articles, essays, and books that exposed the brutal realities of the slave trade. She also became actively involved in various abolitionist organizations, including the American

Anti-Slavery Society, where she worked alongside leading figures such as William Lloyd Garrison and Frederick Douglass.

Despite her growing prominence as an abolitionist, Lydia faced persecution and opposition from those who sought to maintain the status quo. She was subjected to threats and harassment, and her books were banned in some parts of the country. But Lydia refused to be silenced, and she continued to speak out against injustice with unwavering courage and conviction.

In addition to her work as an abolitionist, Lydia was also a vocal advocate for women's rights. She believed strongly in the need for women to have a voice in society and fought tirelessly for their right to vote and participate in the political process.

In 1841, Lydia published "Letters from New York," a collection of essays that tackled a wide range of social and political issues, including women's rights and the abolition of slavery. The book was a critical success and helped to cement Lydia's reputation as one of the leading voices of her generation.

Throughout her life, Lydia remained steadfast in her commitment to justice and equality. She continued to fight for the rights of African Americans and women until her dying breath, leaving behind a legacy that continues to inspire generations of activists to this day.

Lydia Maria Child passed away on October 20, 1880, but her spirit lives on in the countless individuals whose lives have been touched by her courage, her conviction, and her unwavering dedication to the cause of justice. Today, she is remembered as a trailblazer, a visionary, and a true pioneer in the fight for social justice.

Harriet Beecher Stowe

Author of Uncle Tom's Cabin

"Eyes that have never wept cannot comprehend sorrow"

Harriet Beecher Stowe (1811-1896): Stowe was an author best known for her novel "Uncle Tom's Cabin," which had a significant impact on the abolitionist movement. Her book helped to raise awareness about the horrors of slavery.

Harriet Elizabeth Beecher was born on June 14, 1811, in Litchfield, Connecticut, into a family that would become one of the most influential in American history. Her father, Lyman Beecher, was a prominent Congregationalist minister and social reformer, while her mother, Roxana Foote Beecher, was a devoutly religious woman who instilled in her children a deep sense of morality and compassion.

From a young age, Harriet showed a keen intellect and a talent for writing, penning stories and poems that reflected her curiosity about the world around her. Encouraged by her parents, she continued to nurture her passion for literature and education, eventually attending the Hartford Female Seminary, where she honed her writing skills under the tutelage of Catharine Beecher, her older sister.

In 1832, Harriet married Calvin Ellis Stowe, a prominent clergyman and educator, with whom she would have seven children. Despite the demands of motherhood, Harriet continued to write, publishing articles and stories in various magazines and journals.

It was not until 1851, however, that Harriet would achieve literary immortality with the publication of her most famous work, "Uncle Tom's Cabin." The novel, which tells the story of the enslaved African American man Uncle Tom and the horrors of slavery, struck a chord with readers across the country and around the world.

"Uncle Tom's Cabin" had a profound impact on the abolitionist movement, galvanizing public opinion against the institution of slavery and helping to pave the way for its eventual abolition. The book sold over 300,000 copies in its first year alone and was translated into numerous languages, spreading its message of freedom and equality to audiences far and wide.

Despite the book's success, Harriet faced criticism and condemnation from those who opposed her radical ideas. She was accused of exaggerating the horrors of slavery and misrepresenting the South, and her book was banned in some parts of the country. But Harriet refused to be silenced, and she continued to speak out against injustice with unwavering courage and conviction.

In addition to her work as a writer, Harriet was also a vocal advocate for women's rights. She believed strongly in the need for women to have a voice in society and fought tirelessly for their right to vote and participate in the political process.

In 1867, Harriet became one of the founding members of the American Woman Suffrage Association, alongside leading figures such as Susan B. Anthony and Elizabeth Cady Stanton. She also continued to write and speak out on behalf of women's rights, using her platform to amplify the voices of those who had been marginalized and oppressed.

Throughout her life, Harriet remained steadfast in her commitment to justice and equality. She continued to fight for the rights of African Americans and women until her dying breath, leaving behind a legacy that continues to inspire generations of activists to this day.

Harriet Beecher Stowe passed away on July 1, 1896, but her spirit lives on in the countless individuals whose lives have been touched by her courage, her conviction, and her unwavering dedication to the cause of justice. Today, she is remembered as a trailblazer, a visionary, and a true pioneer in the fight for social justice.

Abby Kelley Foster

A Voice for Justice and Equality

Abby Kelley Foster (1811-1887): Foster was a prominent abolitionist and women's rights activist. She was known for her powerful speeches and her tireless advocacy for social reform.

Abby Kelley Foster was born on January 15, 1811, in Pelham, Massachusetts, into a Quaker family with a long tradition of social activism. From an early age, Abby was instilled with a deep sense of morality and a commitment to fighting against injustice and oppression.

Growing up in the early 19th century, Abby witnessed firsthand the horrors of slavery and the injustices faced by women in society. Determined to make a difference, she began speaking out against these injustices at a young age, delivering impassioned speeches on the need for abolition and women's rights.

In 1836, Abby married Stephen Symonds Foster, a fellow abolitionist and reformer, with whom she shared a passion for social justice. Their marriage was marked by mutual respect and admiration, and they worked together as partners in the fight for equality.

As Abby's activism grew, so too did the backlash from those who sought to maintain the status quo. She faced persecution and opposition from those who viewed her advocacy for abolition and women's rights as radical and subversive. But Abby refused to be silenced, and she continued to speak out against injustice with unwavering courage and conviction.

In 1840, Abby became involved in the abolitionist movement in earnest, joining the American Anti-Slavery Society and dedicating herself full-time to the cause of ending slavery. She traveled throughout the country, delivering powerful speeches and organizing rallies to raise awareness about the horrors of slavery and the need for immediate abolition.

Abby's powerful oratory and tireless advocacy made her a leading figure in the abolitionist movement. She was known for her fearlessness in the face of opposition and her unwavering commitment to justice and equality. Her speeches inspired countless individuals to join the fight against slavery and to work towards a more just and equitable society.

In addition to her work as an abolitionist, Abby was also a vocal advocate for women's rights. She believed strongly in the need for women to have a voice in society and fought tirelessly for their right to vote and participate in the political process.

In 1848, Abby attended the Seneca Falls Convention, the first women's rights convention in American history, where she delivered a powerful speech calling for women's suffrage and equal rights under the law. She continued to be actively involved in the women's suffrage movement throughout her life, working alongside leading figures such as Susan B. Anthony and Elizabeth Cady Stanton to secure the right to vote for women.

Despite facing persecution and opposition at every turn, Abby remained steadfast in her commitment to justice and equality. She continued to fight for the rights of African Americans and women until her dying breath, leaving behind a legacy that continues to inspire generations of activists to this day.

Abby Kelley Foster passed away on January 14, 1887, but her spirit lives on in the countless individuals whose lives have been touched by her courage, her conviction, and her unwavering dedication to the cause of justice. Today, she is remembered as a trailblazer, a visionary, and a true pioneer in the fight for social justice.

Amelia Bloomer

Published "The Lily," one of the first newspapers for women

It will not do to say that it is out of woman's sphere to assist in making laws,

for if that were so, then it should be also out of her sphere to submit to them.

Amelia Bloomer (1818-1894): Bloomer was a women's rights advocate and temperance reformer who also supported the abolitionist cause. She published "The Lily," one of the first newspapers for women.

Amelia Jenks Bloomer was born on May 27, 1818, in Homer, New York, into a family of modest means. Raised in a household that valued education and social justice, Amelia was instilled with a deep sense of compassion and a strong belief in the inherent worth and dignity of every individual.

As a young girl, Amelia showed a keen intellect and a passion for learning. Despite the limited educational opportunities available to women at the time, she pursued her studies with determination, devouring books and immersing herself in the world of ideas.

In 1840, at the age of twenty-two, Amelia married Dexter Bloomer, a lawyer and newspaper editor, with whom she would have one son. Their marriage was marked by mutual respect and admiration, and they shared a commitment to social reform and women's rights.

It was not long after her marriage that Amelia began to immerse herself in the world of social reform. Inspired by the teachings of the temperance movement, she became actively involved in the crusade against alcohol consumption, which she saw as a scourge on society.

In 1848, Amelia's life took a dramatic turn when she attended the Seneca Falls Convention, the first women's rights convention in American history. There, she became acquainted with leading figures in the women's rights movement, including Elizabeth Cady Stanton and Lucretia Mott, who would become lifelong friends and allies.

In 1849, Amelia became the editor of "The Lily," one of the first newspapers for women in the United States. Through its pages, she advocated for women's rights, temperance, and other social reforms, using her platform to amplify the voices of those who had been marginalized and oppressed.

One of the most enduring legacies of Amelia's work was her promotion of a new style of dress that came to be known as the "bloomer costume." The costume, which consisted of a knee-length dress worn over full trousers, was designed to provide women with greater freedom of movement and to challenge traditional gender norms.

Despite the ridicule and criticism she faced from those who opposed her radical ideas, Amelia remained undaunted in her quest for justice and equality. She continued to speak out against injustice with unwavering courage and conviction, using her pen and her voice to effect change in society.

In addition to her work as a writer and reformer, Amelia was also a staunch supporter of the abolitionist cause. She believed strongly in the need to end the institution of slavery and worked tirelessly to mobilize public opinion against it.

Throughout her life, Amelia remained committed to the principles of justice and equality. She continued to advocate for women's rights, temperance, and social reform until her dying breath, leaving behind a legacy that continues to inspire generations of activists to this day.

Amelia Bloomer passed away on December 30, 1894, but her spirit lives on in the countless individuals whose lives have been touched by her courage, her conviction, and her unwavering dedication to the cause of justice. Today, she is remembered as a trailblazer, a visionary, and a true pioneer in the fight for women's rights and social reform.

Julia Ward Howe

Author of "The Battle Hymn of the Republic"

"Familiarity so dulls the edge of perception as to make us less acquainted with things forming part of our daily lives"

Julia Ward Howe (1819-1910): Howe was a poet and author best known for writing "The Battle Hymn of the Republic." She was also an abolitionist and women's rights activist.

Julia Ward Howe, born on May 27, 1819, into a prominent New York family, was destined to become one of the most influential figures of her time. Raised in an environment that valued education and social responsibility, Julia was encouraged to pursue her passions and use her talents for the betterment of society.

From a young age, Julia showed a remarkable aptitude for writing and poetry, penning verses that captured the imagination of those around her. Her parents, Samuel Ward and Julia Rush Cutler, recognized her talent and nurtured her love of literature, providing her with the education and support she needed to flourish.

In 1843, Julia married Samuel Gridley Howe, a prominent physician and abolitionist, with whom she would have six children. Their marriage was marked by mutual respect and admiration, and they shared a commitment to social justice and reform.

It was not long after her marriage that Julia's life took a dramatic turn when she became involved in the abolitionist movement. Inspired by the teachings of her husband and other leading abolitionists of the time, she began to speak out against the evils of slavery and to advocate for its immediate abolition.

In 1861, Julia penned what would become her most famous work, "The Battle Hymn of the Republic." The poem, set to the tune of "John

Brown's Body," became an anthem of the Union Army during the Civil War and a rallying cry for the abolitionist cause.

"The Battle Hymn of the Republic" captured the nation's imagination and helped to galvanize public opinion against the institution of slavery. Its powerful imagery and stirring language inspired countless individuals to join the fight for freedom and equality, earning Julia widespread acclaim as a poet and author.

Despite her success as a writer, Julia's activism did not end with the abolition of slavery. She continued to be actively involved in various social reform movements, including the women's suffrage movement.

In 1868, Julia helped to found the New England Women's Club, a pioneering organization dedicated to promoting women's rights and social reform. She also became actively involved in the women's suffrage movement, working alongside leading figures such as Susan B. Anthony and Elizabeth Cady Stanton to secure the right to vote for women.

Throughout her life, Julia faced persecution and opposition from those who sought to maintain the status quo. She was subjected to ridicule and criticism for her radical ideas and outspoken advocacy, but she refused to be silenced. She continued to speak out against injustice with unwavering courage and conviction, using her platform to effect change in society.

Julia Ward Howe passed away on October 17, 1910, but her spirit lives on in the countless individuals whose lives have been touched by her courage, her conviction, and her unwavering dedication to the cause of justice. Today, she is remembered as a trailblazer, a visionary, and a true pioneer in the fight for freedom and equality.

Antoinette Brown Blackwell

First woman to be ordained as a minister in the United States

Antoinette Brown Blackwell (1825-1921): Blackwell was the first woman to be ordained as a minister in the United States. She was also active in the abolitionist and women's rights movements.

Antoinette Louisa Brown was born on May 20, 1825, in Henrietta, New York, into a devoutly religious family with a strong commitment to social justice and equality. Raised in an environment that valued education and moral integrity, Antoinette was encouraged to pursue her passions and strive for excellence in all aspects of her life.

From a young age, Antoinette showed a keen intellect and a deep sense of compassion for those less fortunate than herself. She was deeply influenced by her father's progressive views on religion and his belief in the equality of all people, regardless of race or gender.

In 1845, at the age of twenty, Antoinette enrolled at Oberlin College, a pioneering institution that admitted both men and women and was known for its commitment to social reform. It was there that she first became involved in the abolitionist movement and began to question the traditional roles assigned to women in society.

After graduating from Oberlin in 1847, Antoinette felt a calling to pursue a career in ministry. Despite facing opposition from those who believed that women were not suited for such roles, she remained undaunted in her determination to follow her calling.

In 1850, Antoinette became the first woman to be ordained as a minister in the United States, a groundbreaking achievement that paved the way for future generations of women in the clergy. Her ordination caused controversy and condemnation from some quarters, but Antoinette remained steadfast in her belief that women had a right to pursue careers in ministry.

As a minister, Antoinette was known for her powerful sermons and her unwavering commitment to social justice. She used her platform to advocate for the abolition of slavery, women's rights, and other progressive causes, earning her a reputation as one of the leading voices of her generation.

In 1856, Antoinette married Samuel Blackwell, a prominent abolitionist and reformer, with whom she shared a deep commitment to social justice and equality. Their marriage was marked by mutual respect and admiration, and they worked together as partners in the fight for justice and reform.

Throughout her life, Antoinette remained actively involved in the abolitionist and women's rights movements. She attended conferences and conventions, delivered speeches and lectures, and authored articles and essays advocating for the rights of women and marginalized communities.

In 1869, Antoinette became involved in the women's suffrage movement, working alongside leading figures such as Susan B. Anthony and Elizabeth Cady Stanton to secure the right to vote for women. She believed strongly in the need for women to have a voice in society and fought tirelessly for their right to participate in the political process.

Despite facing persecution and opposition from those who sought to maintain the status quo, Antoinette remained steadfast in her commitment to justice and equality. She continued to speak out against injustice with unwavering courage and conviction, leaving behind a legacy that continues to inspire generations of activists to this day.

Antoinette Brown Blackwell passed away on November 5, 1921, but her spirit lives on in the countless individuals whose lives have been touched by her courage, her conviction, and her unwavering dedication to the cause of justice. Today, she is remembered as a trailblazer, a visionary, and a true pioneer in the fight for equality and social justice.

Maria Weston Chapman

"We may draw good out of evil; we must not do evil, that good may come"

Maria Weston Chapman, born on July 25, 1806, in Weymouth, Massachusetts, was destined to become one of the most influential figures in the abolitionist movement of the 19th century. Raised in a family deeply committed to social justice and reform, Maria was instilled with a sense of moral responsibility and a fervent belief in the inherent dignity and equality of all people.

Maria's upbringing was marked by tragedy and hardship. Her father, Warren Weston, died when she was just four years old, leaving her mother, Anne Strong Weston, to raise Maria and her three siblings alone. Despite the challenges they faced, Anne instilled in her children a love of learning and a commitment to making the world a better place.

From a young age, Maria showed a remarkable intellect and a passion for social justice. She was deeply influenced by her mother's strong abolitionist beliefs and her commitment to the anti-slavery cause. Inspired by her mother's example, Maria became actively involved in the abolitionist movement at a young age, attending meetings and rallies and speaking out against the evils of slavery.

In 1830, Maria married Henry Grafton Chapman, a prominent lawyer and abolitionist, with whom she would have six children. Their marriage was marked by mutual respect and admiration, and they shared a commitment to social justice and reform.

In 1832, Maria became involved in the Boston Female Anti-Slavery Society, a pioneering organization dedicated to promoting the abolition of slavery and advancing the rights of African Americans. She quickly rose to prominence within the organization, using her formidable intellect and organizational skills to mobilize support for the anti-slavery cause.

Maria's talents as an organizer and leader were soon recognized by William Lloyd Garrison, the fiery abolitionist and editor of "The Liberator." In 1839, Garrison appointed Maria as the editor of "The Liberty Bell," an anti-slavery annual publication that became one of the most influential voices in the abolitionist movement.

Under Maria's editorship, "The Liberty Bell" became a powerful platform for the abolitionist cause, featuring essays, speeches, and poems by some of the leading figures in the movement. Maria used the publication to highlight the brutal realities of slavery and to mobilize public opinion against the institution.

Despite facing persecution and opposition from those who sought to maintain the status quo, Maria remained undaunted in her commitment to justice and equality. She continued to speak out against injustice with unwavering courage and conviction, using her platform to effect change in society.

In addition to her work as an abolitionist, Maria was also a vocal advocate for women's rights. She believed strongly in the need for women to have a voice in society and fought tirelessly for their right to participate in the political process.

In 1840, Maria attended the World Anti-Slavery Convention in London, where she became the first American woman to address the convention. She used her speech to call for the abolition of slavery and to advocate for the rights of women to participate fully in the anti-slavery movement.

Throughout her life, Maria Weston Chapman remained committed to the principles of justice and equality. She continued to fight for the rights of African Americans and women until her dying breath, leaving behind a legacy that continues to inspire generations of activists to this day.

Maria Weston Chapman passed away on July 12, 1885, but her spirit lives on in the countless individuals whose lives have been touched by her courage, her conviction, and her unwavering dedication to the cause of justice. Today, she is remembered as a trailblazer, a visionary, and a true pioneer in the fight for abolition and social justice.

Sarah Josepha Hale

Editor of the "Ladies' Magazine

Sarah Josepha Hale, born on October 24, 1788, in Newport, New Hampshire, emerged as one of the most influential figures of her time, leaving an indelible mark on American literature and social reform. Raised in a family that valued education and community involvement, Sarah developed a passion for learning and a deep-seated belief in the power of words to effect positive change.

Sarah's early years were marked by tragedy and hardship. Her father, Captain Gordon Buell, died when she was just a young girl, leaving her mother, Martha Whittlesey Buell, to raise Sarah and her siblings alone. Despite the challenges they faced, Martha instilled in her children a love of literature and a sense of moral responsibility.

From a young age, Sarah showed a remarkable talent for writing, penning poems and essays that revealed a keen intellect and a sharp wit. Encouraged by her mother, she began submitting her work to local newspapers and magazines, earning recognition for her literary prowess.

In 1813, Sarah married David Hale, a lawyer and journalist, with whom she would have five children. Their marriage was marked by mutual respect and admiration, and they shared a commitment to social reform and public service.

Throughout her life, Sarah used her platform as a writer and editor to advocate for causes she believed in, including women's education and the abolition of slavery. In 1828, she became the editor of the "Ladies' Magazine," a pioneering publication that provided a forum for women writers and addressed issues of concern to women.

As the editor of the "Ladies' Magazine," Sarah used her influence to promote women's education and to elevate the status of women in society. She believed strongly in the importance of education for women and worked tirelessly to expand educational opportunities for girls and young women.

In addition to her work as an advocate for women's education, Sarah was also a vocal supporter of the abolitionist movement. She used her platform as a writer and editor to raise awareness about the horrors of slavery and to mobilize public opinion against it.

Sarah's most enduring literary legacy is perhaps her poem "Mary Had a Little Lamb," which she wrote in 1830 and published in the "Juvenile Miscellany." The poem, which tells the story of a young girl and her beloved pet lamb, became an instant classic and remains one of the most beloved nursery rhymes in American literature.

Despite her success as a writer and editor, Sarah faced persecution and opposition from those who sought to silence her. She was criticized for her outspoken advocacy on behalf of women and marginalized communities, but she refused to be silenced.

In 1837, Sarah became the editor of "Godey's Lady's Book," a widely popular magazine that became one of the most influential publications of its time. Under Sarah's editorship, "Godey's" featured articles on a wide range of topics, including fashion, cooking, and home décor, as well as literature and social commentary.

Throughout her tenure at "Godey's," Sarah used her influence to promote social reform and to advocate for the rights of women and marginalized communities. She believed strongly in the power of literature to effect positive change and worked tirelessly to use her platform for the greater good.

In addition to her work as an editor, Sarah was also actively involved in various philanthropic endeavors, including the establishment of the first public playground in Philadelphia and the founding of the Seaman's Aid Society, which provided assistance to sailors and their families.

Despite facing criticism and opposition from some quarters, Sarah remained steadfast in her commitment to social reform and public service. She continued to advocate for the rights of women and marginalized communities until her dying breath, leaving behind a legacy that continues to inspire generations of activists and writers.

Sarah Josepha Hale passed away on April 30, 1879, but her spirit lives on in the countless individuals whose lives have been touched by her courage, her conviction, and her unwavering dedication to the cause of justice and equality. Today, she is remembered as a literary luminary, a champion of social reform, and a true pioneer in the fight for women's rights.

Mary Livermore

A Trailblazer for Equality and Justice

Mary Ashton Rice Livermore, born on December 19, 1820, in Boston, Massachusetts, was destined to become one of the most influential figures in the abolitionist and women's rights movements of the 19th century. Raised in a family that valued education and social justice, Mary was instilled with a sense of moral responsibility and a fervent belief in the inherent dignity and equality of all people.

Mary's upbringing was marked by tragedy and hardship. Her father, Timothy Rice, died when she was just six years old, leaving her mother, Hannah Rice, to raise Mary and her five siblings alone. Despite the challenges they faced, Hannah instilled in her children a love of learning and a commitment to making the world a better place.

From a young age, Mary showed a remarkable intellect and a passion for social justice. She was deeply influenced by her mother's strong abolitionist beliefs and her commitment to the anti-slavery cause. Inspired by her mother's example, Mary became actively involved in the abolitionist movement at a young age, attending meetings and rallies and speaking out against the evils of slavery.

In 1845, at the age of twenty-five, Mary married Daniel Parker Livermore, a prominent lawyer and abolitionist, with whom she would have four children. Their marriage was marked by mutual respect and admiration, and they shared a commitment to social justice and reform.

In 1857, Mary's life took a dramatic turn when she became involved in the women's rights movement. Inspired by the teachings of leading figures such as Susan B. Anthony and Elizabeth Cady Stanton, she began to speak out against the injustices faced by women in society and to advocate for their rights.

During the Civil War, Mary put her beliefs into action by volunteering as a nurse for the Union Army. She cared for wounded soldiers on the front lines and worked tirelessly to alleviate their suffering, earning her a reputation as a compassionate and dedicated caregiver.

After the war, Mary became increasingly involved in the women's rights movement, working alongside leading figures such as Susan B. Anthony and Elizabeth Cady Stanton to secure the right to vote for women. She believed strongly in the need for women to have a voice in society and fought tirelessly for their right to participate in the political process.

In 1869, Mary helped to found the American Woman Suffrage Association, a pioneering organization dedicated to promoting women's rights and social reform. She also became actively involved in the women's suffrage movement, delivering speeches and lectures across the country to mobilize support for the cause.

Throughout her life, Mary faced persecution and opposition from those who sought to maintain the status quo. She was subjected to ridicule and criticism for her radical ideas and outspoken advocacy, but she refused to be silenced. She continued to speak out against injustice with unwavering courage and conviction, using her platform to effect change in society.

In addition to her work as a women's rights activist, Mary was also a vocal advocate for the abolition of slavery. She believed strongly in the need to end the institution of slavery and worked tirelessly to mobilize public opinion against it.

Mary Livermore passed away on May 23, 1905, but her spirit lives on in the countless individuals whose lives have been touched by her courage, her conviction, and her unwavering dedication to the cause of justice. Today, she is remembered as a trailblazer, a visionary, and a true pioneer in the fight for abolition and women's rights.

Susan Paul

A Voice for Freedom and Equality

Susan Paul, born on March 3, 1805, into a Quaker family in Pennsylvania, emerged as a prominent figure in the abolitionist movement of the 19th century. Raised in a community that prioritized social justice and equality, Susan was instilled with a deep sense of compassion and a fervent belief in the inherent dignity and worth of all individuals.

Susan's upbringing was rooted in the principles of the Quaker faith, which emphasized peace, equality, and the abolition of slavery. From a young age, she was taught to challenge injustice and to speak out against oppression, values that would shape her activism in the years to come.

As a young woman, Susan became increasingly involved in the abolitionist movement, inspired by the teachings of leading figures such as William Lloyd Garrison and Lucretia Mott. She attended meetings and rallies, participated in protests and demonstrations, and used her voice to advocate for the immediate abolition of slavery.

In 1825, at the age of twenty, Susan married Thomas Paul, a fellow Quaker and abolitionist, with whom she would have three children. Their marriage was marked by mutual respect and shared values, and they worked together as partners in the fight against slavery and injustice.

Susan's activism extended beyond her personal relationships, as she became actively involved in various abolitionist organizations and societies. She participated in the Pennsylvania Anti-Slavery Society and the Philadelphia Female Anti-Slavery Society, using her organizational skills and passion for justice to advance the cause of freedom.

Throughout her life, Susan faced persecution and opposition from those who sought to maintain the status quo. As an outspoken abolitionist in a society deeply divided over the issue of slavery, she was subjected to ridicule and criticism, and her activism often put her at odds with family members and community members who did not share her views.

Despite the challenges she faced, Susan remained steadfast in her commitment to justice and equality. She continued to speak out against slavery with unwavering courage and conviction, using her platform to effect change in society.

In addition to her work as an abolitionist, Susan was also a vocal advocate for women's rights. She believed strongly in the need for women to have a voice in society and fought tirelessly for their right to participate in the political process.

Although the women's suffrage movement had not yet gained widespread momentum during Susan's lifetime, she laid the groundwork for future generations of activists by advocating for women's equality and empowerment.

Susan Paul passed away on December 14, 1849, but her legacy lives on in the countless individuals whose lives have been touched by her courage, her conviction, and her unwavering dedication to the cause of justice. Today, she is remembered as a trailblazer, a visionary, and a true pioneer in the fight for freedom and equality.

Ellen Craft

A Brave Journey to Freedom

Ellen Craft, born on November 6, 1826, into the bonds of slavery in Clinton, Georgia, emerged as a symbol of courage and resilience in the fight against oppression. Her life's journey from bondage to freedom is a testament to the indomitable human spirit and the unwavering quest for justice.

Ellen's early childhood was marked by the harsh realities of slavery. Born to Maria, an enslaved woman, and her white enslaver, Ellen's life was shaped by the brutal system of chattel slavery that denied her basic human rights and dignity. Despite the hardships she endured, Ellen's spirit remained unbroken, and she yearned for freedom.

As Ellen grew older, she formed a bond with another enslaved person, William Craft, who would become her husband and partner in the quest for freedom. Together, Ellen and William hatched a daring plan to escape from bondage and seek refuge in the North, where slavery was outlawed.

In December 1848, Ellen and William embarked on their perilous journey to freedom. With Ellen disguising herself as a white man and William posing as her enslaved servant, they traveled by train and steamship, navigating through hostile territory and evading capture at every turn.

Their journey was fraught with danger, but Ellen and William remained undaunted in their determination to reach freedom. Their courage and resourcefulness were put to the test as they faced countless obstacles and challenges along the way.

After a harrowing journey of nearly a thousand miles, Ellen and William finally reached the safety of Philadelphia, where they were welcomed by abolitionists and sympathizers who admired their bravery and resilience. Their escape sent shockwaves throughout the country and became a rallying cry for the abolitionist cause.

In the North, Ellen and William became active participants in the abolitionist movement, using their firsthand experience of slavery to educate others about its horrors and advocate for its abolition. They traveled across the country, speaking at rallies and meetings, and sharing their story of courage and resistance.

Ellen, in particular, emerged as a powerful voice for freedom and equality. Her eloquent speeches and impassioned pleas inspired countless individuals to join the fight against slavery and work towards a more just and equitable society.

Despite their newfound freedom, Ellen and William continued to face persecution and discrimination as they navigated life in the North. They were subjected to racist attitudes and stereotypes, and struggled to find employment and housing in a society still deeply divided along racial lines.

In addition to their work as abolitionists, Ellen and William also became active participants in the women's suffrage movement. They recognized the interconnectedness of struggles for freedom and equality, and lent their support to the fight for women's rights.

Ellen Craft passed away on September 7, 1897, but her legacy lives on in the countless individuals whose lives have been touched by her courage, her resilience, and her unwavering commitment to the cause of justice. Today, she is remembered as a trailblazer, a visionary, and a true hero in the fight against oppression and injustice.

Emily Howland

A Pioneer in Abolitionism and Women's Rights

Emily Howland, a remarkable figure in American history, dedicated her life to the causes of abolitionism and women's suffrage. Born in 1827 and living until 1929, she witnessed and contributed to significant social and political changes in the United States. This essay will explore the life of Emily Howland, focusing on her early childhood, her activism in the anti-slavery movement, her involvement in the women's suffrage movement, and her enduring legacy.

Early Childhood and Education:

Emily Howland was born on November 25, 1827, in Sherwood, New York, to a Quaker family with a strong commitment to social justice and equality. Raised in a supportive environment, Howland's upbringing instilled in her the values of compassion, empathy, and the importance of education. She received a formal education at a Quaker school, where she excelled academically and developed a deep-seated passion for learning.

Marriages:

Unlike many women of her time, Emily Howland never married. Instead, she devoted her life to her work as an abolitionist, educator, and advocate for women's rights. Her decision to remain unmarried allowed her the freedom to pursue her passions and dedicate herself fully to social reform.

Activism in the Anti-Slavery Movement:

Emily Howland's involvement in the abolitionist movement began at a young age. Inspired by her Quaker faith and the teachings of her family, she became increasingly aware of the injustices of slavery and felt compelled to take action. Howland used her privilege and resources to support the anti-slavery cause, providing financial assistance to organizations working to end slavery and supporting the Underground Railroad.

In addition to her financial contributions, Howland actively participated in anti-slavery meetings, lectures, and rallies, where she advocated for the immediate emancipation of enslaved individuals and the rights of African Americans. Her tireless efforts made her a respected and influential figure within the abolitionist movement.

Involvement in the Women's Suffrage Movement:

As the abolitionist movement gained momentum, Emily Howland recognized the interconnectedness of social justice causes and became involved in the women's suffrage movement. She believed strongly in the equality of all individuals, regardless of gender, and advocated for women's right to vote.

Howland's involvement in the women's suffrage movement included attending suffrage conventions, signing petitions, and advocating for legislative reforms that would grant women the right to vote. She understood that political empowerment was essential for achieving gender equality and worked tirelessly to advance the cause of women's suffrage.

Persecution and Challenges:

Throughout her life, Emily Howland faced opposition and persecution for her beliefs and activism. As an outspoken abolitionist and advocate for women's rights, she encountered resistance from those who opposed social reform and sought to maintain the status quo. Howland's commitment to her principles, however, remained unwavering, and she continued to fight for justice despite the challenges she faced.

Participation in Women's Voting Rights Processes:

Emily Howland played an active role in the women's voting rights processes of her time. She attended suffrage conventions, participated in suffrage rallies and protests, and worked alongside other suffragists to advocate for women's right to vote. Howland understood the importance of political engagement and believed that women's voices deserved to be heard in the democratic process.

Legacy:

Emily Howland's legacy as an abolitionist, educator, and advocate for women's rights lives on today. Her tireless efforts to combat injustice and inequality continue to inspire generations of activists and advocates. Howland's commitment to social justice serves as a reminder of the power of individuals to effect change and make a difference in the world.

Conclusion:

Emily Howland's life and work exemplify the values of compassion, empathy, and social responsibility. Her dedication to the causes of abolitionism and women's suffrage serves as an enduring example of courage, resilience, and commitment to justice. As we reflect on her legacy, let us honor her memory by continuing to work towards a more just, equitable, and inclusive society for all.

Hannah More

A Beacon of Enlightenment and Compassion

Hannah More (1745-1833): More was a British writer and philanthropist who supported various social causes, including the abolition of slavery. She wrote anti-slavery pamphlets and campaigned for abolition.

Hannah More, born on February 2, 1745, in Stapleton, Gloucestershire, England, was a woman ahead of her time. As a prolific writer, philanthropist, and social reformer, she left an indelible mark on British society, advocating for the abolition of slavery and championing various other social causes. Her life's work serves as a testament to the power of compassion, enlightenment, and activism in the face of oppression and injustice.

Early Life and Education:

Hannah was the fourth of five daughters born to Jacob More, a schoolmaster, and his wife, Mary. Raised in a devoutly religious household, she received a basic education at her father's school, where she developed a lifelong love of learning and literature. Despite the limited educational opportunities available to women at the time, Hannah's parents encouraged her intellectual pursuits and nurtured her talents as a writer and thinker.

Marriage and Writing Career:

In 1767, at the age of twenty-two, Hannah moved to London with her sisters to pursue a career as a writer. She quickly gained recognition for her literary talents and became a prominent figure in London's intellectual circles. In 1774, she published her first book of poetry, "The Inflexible Captive," which garnered critical acclaim and established her reputation as a writer.

Throughout the 1770s and 1780s, Hannah continued to write prolifically, producing a wide range of works, including plays, essays, and educational literature. Her writing was characterized by its moral earnestness and social conscience, reflecting her deep concern for the welfare of society's most vulnerable members.

Abolitionist Activism:

In the late 1780s, Hannah became increasingly involved in the abolitionist movement, inspired by the writings of leading abolitionists such as William Wilberforce and Thomas Clarkson. She was deeply troubled by the horrors of the transatlantic slave trade and felt a moral obligation to speak out against it.

Hannah used her platform as a writer to raise awareness about the evils of slavery and to advocate for its abolition. In 1788, she published "Slavery: A Poem," a powerful and impassioned anti-slavery poem that drew attention to the suffering endured by enslaved Africans and called for an end to the slave trade.

In addition to her poetry, Hannah also wrote several anti-slavery pamphlets and tracts, including "Thoughts on the Importance of the Manners of the Great to General Society" and "An Estimate of the Religion of the Fashionable World." These works sought to challenge prevailing attitudes towards slavery and to persuade readers of the moral imperative of abolition.

Philanthropic Endeavors:

In addition to her abolitionist activism, Hannah was also deeply committed to philanthropy and social reform. She was actively involved in various charitable organizations and initiatives aimed at alleviating poverty, promoting education, and improving the moral and spiritual welfare of society.

One of Hannah's most notable philanthropic endeavors was her involvement in the establishment of Sunday schools for the education of poor children. Alongside her friend and fellow reformer, William Wilberforce, she played a key role in promoting the Sunday school movement and expanding access to education for underprivileged youth.

Persecution and Opposition:

Despite her noble intentions and tireless efforts on behalf of the oppressed, Hannah faced considerable opposition and criticism from conservative elements within British society. She was denounced as a radical and a troublemaker by those who sought to maintain the status quo and resist social change.

Hannah's outspoken advocacy for abolition and her critique of societal norms and institutions made her a target for attacks and smear campaigns from her detractors. She endured slander, ridicule, and even threats to her personal safety, but she remained steadfast in her commitment to the cause of justice and equality.

Women's Rights:

While Hannah's primary focus was on the abolition of slavery, she also expressed support for women's rights and equality. Although she did not actively participate in the women's suffrage movement, she believed in the importance of women's education and empowerment and advocated for their social and intellectual advancement.

Legacy:

Hannah More passed away on September 7, 1833, at the age of eighty-eight, but her legacy lives on in the countless individuals whose lives have been touched by her compassion, wisdom, and courage. She is remembered as a pioneering figure in the fight against slavery and a beacon of enlightenment and compassion in an age of darkness and oppression. Today, her contributions to the abolitionist movement continue to inspire generations of activists and advocates for social justice and human rights.

Anne Knight

British Voice for Equality and Truth

Anne Knight, born on November 2, 1786, in Chelmsford, Essex, England, emerged as a pioneering figure in the fight for social reform and human rights in 19th-century Britain. Through her tireless activism and unwavering commitment to justice, she left an indelible mark on the abolitionist movement and the struggle for women's rights, laying the groundwork for generations of activists to come.

Early Life and Education:

Anne was the daughter of John Knight, a wealthy landowner, and his wife, Mary. Raised in a privileged household, she received a comprehensive education, which was uncommon for women of her time. Anne's upbringing instilled in her a strong sense of social responsibility and a fervent belief in the equality of all people.

Marriage and Family Life:

In 1807, at the age of twenty-one, Anne married Edward Smith, a Quaker grocer and social reformer. The couple shared a deep commitment to social justice and spent their married life advocating for the rights of the oppressed and marginalized.

Together, Anne and Edward had several children, whom they raised in an environment that valued compassion, empathy, and a sense of duty to one's fellow human beings. Their family life provided a strong foundation for Anne's later activism and inspired her to dedicate herself to the pursuit of social reform.

Involvement in the Anti-Slavery Movement:

Anne's involvement in the anti-slavery movement began in the early 1820s, inspired by the writings and speeches of leading abolitionists such as William Wilberforce and Thomas Clarkson. She was deeply troubled by the horrors of the transatlantic slave trade and felt compelled to take action against this grave injustice.

Anne joined the Female Society for Birmingham, which was dedicated to promoting the abolition of slavery and improving the conditions of enslaved people in the British colonies. She participated in protests, signed petitions, and distributed anti-slavery literature, using her voice and influence to raise awareness about the evils of slavery.

Persecution and Opposition:

Anne's activism brought her into conflict with the conservative forces of British society, who sought to maintain the status quo and resist social change. She faced persecution and harassment from her detractors, who viewed her as a threat to their vested interests and sought to silence her voice.

Despite the opposition she faced, Anne remained steadfast in her commitment to justice and equality. She refused to be intimidated or deterred by the obstacles in her path, continuing to advocate for the abolition of slavery with unwavering courage and conviction.

Involvement in Women's Rights:

In addition to her work in the anti-slavery movement, Anne was also a vocal advocate for women's rights and equality. She believed strongly in the need for women to have a voice in society and fought tirelessly for their right to participate fully in the political process.

Anne was actively involved in the women's suffrage movement, working alongside leading figures such as Millicent Fawcett and Emily Pankhurst to secure the right to vote for women. She organized rallies, gave speeches, and lobbied politicians, using her platform to mobilize support for the cause of women's suffrage.

Legacy:

Anne Knight passed away on October 4, 1862, but her legacy lives on in the countless individuals whose lives have been touched by her courage, her conviction, and her unwavering dedication to the cause of justice.

Today, she is remembered as a trailblazer, a visionary, and a true pioneer in the fight for abolition and women's rights. Her contributions to the struggle for social reform continue to inspire and motivate activists around the world.

Elizabeth Heyrick

A Tireless Advocate for Immediate Emancipation

Elizabeth Heyrick, born on December 9, 1769, in Leicester, England, emerged as a fearless and uncompromising voice in the fight against slavery in 19th-century Britain. Through her passionate advocacy and unwavering commitment to justice, she became a leading figure in the abolitionist movement, pioneering the call for the immediate and unconditional emancipation of enslaved people.

Early Life and Education:

Elizabeth was the daughter of Thomas and Ann Coltman, members of the Society of Friends (Quakers), who instilled in her a strong sense of moral responsibility and a commitment to social justice. Raised in a household that valued education and enlightenment, Elizabeth received a comprehensive education, which included instruction in literature, history, and philosophy.

Marriage and Family Life:

In 1794, at the age of twenty-five, Elizabeth married John Heyrick, a Quaker grocer and social reformer. The couple shared a deep commitment to the principles of equality and justice, and their marriage provided a strong foundation for Elizabeth's later activism.

Although Elizabeth and John had no children of their own, they devoted themselves to supporting and nurturing the welfare of others, particularly those who were oppressed and marginalized. Their home became a gathering place for like-minded individuals, where ideas were exchanged, and plans for social reform were hatched.

Involvement in the Anti-Slavery Movement:

Elizabeth's involvement in the anti-slavery movement began in the early 1820s, inspired by the writings and speeches of leading abolitionists such as William Wilberforce and Thomas Clarkson. She was deeply troubled by the horrors of the transatlantic slave trade and felt compelled to take action against this grave injustice.

In 1824, Elizabeth published her seminal work, "Immediate not Gradual Abolition," in which she made a powerful and impassioned case for the immediate and unconditional emancipation of enslaved people. Rejecting the idea of gradual emancipation as insufficient and morally bankrupt, she called for decisive action to end the institution of slavery once and for all.

Elizabeth's pamphlet caused a sensation in abolitionist circles and galvanized support for the cause of immediate emancipation. Her uncompromising stance challenged prevailing attitudes towards slavery and forced abolitionists to confront the moral imperative of ending the institution without delay.

Persecution and Opposition:

Elizabeth's advocacy for immediate emancipation brought her into conflict with the conservative forces of British society, who sought to maintain the status quo and resist social change. She faced persecution and harassment from her detractors, who viewed her as a threat to their vested interests and sought to silence her voice.

Despite the opposition she faced, Elizabeth remained steadfast in her commitment to justice and equality. She refused to be intimidated or deterred by the obstacles in her path, continuing to advocate for the immediate abolition of slavery with unwavering courage and conviction.

Involvement in Women's Rights:

In addition to her work in the anti-slavery movement, Elizabeth was also a vocal advocate for women's rights and equality. She believed strongly in the need for women to have a voice in society and fought tirelessly for their right to participate fully in the political process.

Although she did not actively participate in the women's suffrage movement, Elizabeth supported the cause of women's rights and used her platform as a writer and activist to promote gender equality and empowerment.

Legacy:

Elizabeth Heyrick passed away on December 8, 1831, but her legacy lives on in the countless individuals whose lives have been touched by her courage, her conviction, and her unwavering dedication to the cause of justice. Today, she is remembered as a trailblazer, a visionary, and a true pioneer in the fight for abolition and women's rights. Her contributions to the struggle for social reform continue to inspire and motivate activists around the world.

Mary Prince

The Voice of Resistance and Resilience

Mary Prince, born around 1788 in Bermuda, emerged as a powerful advocate for the abolition of slavery and a prominent autobiographer whose writings shed light on the brutal realities of enslavement in the Caribbean. Through her courageous storytelling and unwavering determination, she became a beacon of hope for oppressed people everywhere, leaving an indelible mark on the history of abolitionism.

Early Life and Enslavement:

Mary's early life was marked by the harsh realities of slavery in the British Caribbean. Born into bondage on a plantation in Bermuda, she endured unimaginable hardship and cruelty from a young age. Separated from her family and subjected to backbreaking labor, Mary's childhood was defined by exploitation and abuse at the hands of her enslavers.

As she grew older, Mary was bought and sold multiple times, enduring the horrors of plantation life under different masters. She witnessed firsthand the brutal treatment inflicted upon enslaved people, including beatings, starvation, and forced labor in the fields. Despite the dehumanizing conditions of her enslavement, Mary never lost her spirit of resilience or her determination to be free.

Marriage and Family:

In her early twenties, Mary formed a relationship with a fellow enslaved man named Daniel James, whom she married in a ceremony not recognized by the law. Their union provided solace and support in the face of adversity, as they navigated the challenges of slavery together. However, their happiness was short-lived, as they were soon separated by the cruel whims of their enslavers.

Persecution and Resistance:

Throughout her life, Mary faced persecution and punishment for daring to resist the injustices of slavery. She endured beatings, starvation, and other forms of physical and emotional abuse at the hands of her enslavers, who sought to crush her spirit and maintain their control over her. Despite the risks, Mary remained steadfast in her defiance, refusing to accept the dehumanization and degradation imposed upon her.

In 1828, Mary made the courageous decision to escape from her enslavers and seek freedom. With the help of sympathetic individuals, she fled to London, where she found refuge with abolitionist allies who supported her in her quest for emancipation. Her escape marked a turning point in her life, as she embraced her newfound freedom and resolved to use her voice to speak out against the evils of slavery.

Autobiography and Activism:

In 1831, Mary's powerful autobiography, "The History of Mary Prince, A West Indian Slave," was published in London. In her memoir, she recounted her experiences of enslavement with searing honesty and raw emotion, exposing the brutal realities of life under the system of chattel slavery. Her narrative captivated readers and helped to galvanize support for the abolitionist cause, as people across Britain and beyond were moved by her harrowing tale of survival and resilience.

Mary's autobiography played a crucial role in raising awareness about the brutality of slavery and generating public support for its abolition. Her firsthand account provided a powerful testament to the humanity and dignity of enslaved people, challenging the dehumanizing stereotypes and narratives perpetuated by proponents of slavery.

Legacy:

Mary Prince passed away in obscurity around 1833, but her legacy lives on in the hearts and minds of people around the world. Her courageous resistance to oppression and her unwavering commitment to justice continue to inspire generations of activists and advocates for human rights. Today, she is remembered as a trailblazer in the fight against slavery and a symbol of hope and resilience for oppressed people everywhere.

Mary Ann McCracken

A Champion for Justice in Ireland

Mary Ann McCracken, born on July 8, 1770, in Belfast, Ireland, emerged as a prominent Irish abolitionist and social reformer in the 19th century. Through her tireless activism and unwavering commitment to justice, she became a leading voice in the fight against slavery and a champion for the rights of the oppressed. Her life's work serves as a testament to the power of courage, compassion, and resilience in the face of injustice.

Early Life and Education:

Mary Ann was the youngest daughter of Captain John McCracken, a successful shipowner, and Ann Joy, a woman of strong moral character and social conscience. Raised in a household that valued education and enlightenment, Mary Ann received a comprehensive education, which included instruction in literature, history, and philosophy. Her parents instilled in her a deep sense of empathy and compassion for the less fortunate, teaching her to use her privilege for the betterment of society.

Marriage and Family Life:

Mary Ann never married, choosing instead to devote her life to the pursuit of social justice and reform. She remained close to her family throughout her life, particularly her older brother Henry Joy McCracken, a prominent United Irishman and revolutionary. Their shared commitment to the cause of Irish independence and social justice forged a strong bond between them, as they worked together to advance the principles of liberty, equality, and fraternity.

Involvement in the Anti-Slavery Movement:

Mary Ann's involvement in the abolitionist movement began in the early 19th century, inspired by the writings and speeches of leading abolitionists such as William Wilberforce and Thomas Clarkson. She was deeply troubled by the horrors of the transatlantic slave trade and felt compelled to take action against this grave injustice.

In 1800, Mary Ann became a founding member of the Belfast Ladies' Anti-Slavery Society, one of the first organizations of its kind in Ireland dedicated to promoting the abolition of slavery. She played a leading role in the society, organizing lectures, fundraising events, and petition drives to raise awareness about the plight of enslaved people and to advocate for their emancipation.

Persecution and Opposition:

Mary Ann's activism brought her into conflict with the conservative forces of Irish society, who sought to maintain the status quo and resist social change. She faced persecution and harassment from her detractors, who viewed her as a threat to their vested interests and sought to silence her voice.

Despite the opposition she faced, Mary Ann remained steadfast in her commitment to justice and equality. She refused to be intimidated or deterred by the obstacles in her path, continuing to advocate for the abolition of slavery with unwavering courage and conviction.

Involvement in Women's Rights:

In addition to her work in the abolitionist movement, Mary Ann was also a supporter of women's rights and gender equality. Although she did not actively participate in the women's suffrage movement, she believed strongly in the need for women to have a voice in society and to be treated as equals.

Mary Ann used her platform as an abolitionist and social reformer to advocate for women's rights, challenging the traditional gender roles and stereotypes that confined women to the domestic sphere. She believed that women had a vital role to play in the fight for social justice and urged them to assert their rights and demand equal treatment under the law.

Legacy:

Mary Ann McCracken passed away on July 26, 1866, but her legacy lives on in the hearts and minds of people around the world. She is remembered as a pioneering figure in the abolitionist movement and a trailblazer in the fight against oppression and injustice. Her tireless activism and unwavering commitment to justice continue to inspire generations of activists and advocates for human rights, both in Ireland and beyond.

Jane Grey Swisshelm

A Pen of Conviction and Courage

Jane Grey Swisshelm, born on December 6, 1815, in Pittsburgh, Pennsylvania, emerged as a pioneering journalist, abolitionist, and women's rights advocate in 19th-century America. Through her fearless journalism and unwavering commitment to justice, she became a leading voice in the fight against slavery and a champion for the rights of women. Her life's work serves as a testament to the power of conviction, courage, and perseverance in the face of oppression and adversity.

Early Life and Education:

Jane was born into a middle-class family in Pittsburgh, Pennsylvania, where she spent her formative years surrounded by books, ideas, and discussions about social justice. Her parents, John and Jane Grey, instilled in her a love of learning and a strong sense of moral responsibility, which would shape her future as a writer and activist.

Despite facing financial hardship after her father's death when she was just eleven years old, Jane was determined to pursue an education and make a difference in the world. She attended local schools in Pittsburgh and later enrolled in the Pittsburgh Female Seminary, where she received a rigorous education in literature, history, and philosophy.

Marriage and Family Life:

In 1836, at the age of twenty-one, Jane married James Swisshelm, a lawyer and abolitionist who shared her passion for social reform. Their marriage was marked by mutual respect, shared values, and a deep commitment to the principles of justice and equality. Together, they supported each other's endeavors and worked tirelessly to advance the cause of abolition and women's rights.

Throughout their marriage, Jane and James faced numerous challenges and hardships, including financial struggles and social ostracism from their conservative peers. Despite the obstacles in their path, they remained steadfast in their convictions and dedicated themselves to the pursuit of social justice and reform.

Involvement in the Anti-Slavery Movement:

Jane's involvement in the abolitionist movement began in the 1840s, inspired by the writings and speeches of leading abolitionists such as Frederick Douglass and William Lloyd Garrison. She was deeply troubled by the horrors of slavery and felt a moral obligation to speak out against this grave injustice.

In 1848, Jane became a contributing writer for the anti-slavery newspaper The Pittsburgh Saturday Visitor, where she used her platform to advocate for the immediate and unconditional emancipation of enslaved people. Her fearless journalism and uncompromising stance on abolitionism made her a target of criticism and hostility from pro-slavery forces, but she refused to be silenced or intimidated by their attacks.

Persecution and Opposition:

As an outspoken abolitionist and journalist, Jane faced persecution and opposition from those who sought to defend the institution of slavery and uphold the status quo. She endured criticism, ridicule, and threats to her personal safety, but remained steadfast in her commitment to justice and equality.

In 1850, Jane's anti-slavery activism brought her into conflict with the Democratic Party establishment in Pennsylvania, who sought to suppress her efforts to expose the complicity of party leaders in the perpetuation of slavery. She was expelled from the party and subjected to smear campaigns and character assassination attempts, but she refused to back down or compromise her principles.

Involvement in Women's Rights:

In addition to her work in the abolitionist movement, Jane was also a vocal advocate for women's rights and gender equality. She believed strongly in the need for women to have a voice in society and to be treated as equals.

In 1851, Jane attended the Women's Rights Convention in Akron, Ohio, where she delivered a powerful speech on the need for women's suffrage and political equality. Her speech, delivered amidst opposition and skepticism from some of the male delegates, electrified the audience and helped to galvanize support for the women's rights movement.

Legacy:

Jane Grey Swisshelm passed away on July 22, 1884, but her legacy lives on in the hearts and minds of people around the world. She is remembered as a pioneering journalist, abolitionist, and women's rights advocate who used her pen to challenge injustice and inspire change. Her fearless journalism and unwavering commitment to justice continue to inspire generations of activists and advocates for social reform, both in America and beyond.

Matilda Joslyn Gage

A Crusader for Women's Rights and Abolition

Matilda Joslyn Gage, born on March 24, 1826, in Cicero, New York, emerged as a towering figure in the women's rights movement and abolitionist cause in the 19th century. Through her unwavering commitment to equality and justice, she became a driving force behind the fight for women's suffrage and the abolition of slavery. Her activism and advocacy continue to inspire generations of activists striving for social change.

Early Life and Education:

Matilda was born into a progressive and intellectually stimulating environment. Her father, Hezekiah Joslyn, was a fervent abolitionist, and her mother, Helen Lesher, instilled in her a strong sense of independence and social responsibility. Growing up, Matilda was exposed to discussions about social justice and equality, laying the foundation for her future activism.

Despite limited formal education for women at the time, Matilda's parents encouraged her intellectual pursuits. She voraciously read books on history, politics, and philosophy, shaping her worldview and fueling her passion for social reform. Matilda's thirst for knowledge and her commitment to justice set her on a path of activism from a young age.

Marriage and Family Life:

In 1845, at the age of nineteen, Matilda married Henry Hill Gage, a businessman and abolitionist. Their marriage was marked by mutual respect and shared values, with Henry supporting Matilda's activism and advocacy for women's rights. Together, they raised five children in a household that valued equality, education, and social justice.

Persecution and Opposition:

Matilda's activism often brought her into conflict with the conservative forces of society, who resisted efforts to challenge the status quo. She faced persecution and opposition from those who sought to maintain traditional gender roles and deny women their rights and freedoms. Despite the obstacles she encountered, Matilda remained undeterred in her pursuit of justice and equality.

Involvement in the Abolitionist Movement:

Matilda's commitment to social reform led her to become actively involved in the abolitionist movement. Inspired by her father's abolitionist beliefs, she joined the fight against slavery, advocating for its immediate and unconditional abolition. Matilda participated in anti-slavery lectures, rallies, and protests, using her voice to amplify the calls for freedom and emancipation.

As a writer and speaker, Matilda contributed to abolitionist newspapers and publications, raising awareness about the brutality of slavery and the moral imperative of its abolition. She believed that the struggle for women's rights and the fight against slavery were interconnected, advocating for the rights and dignity of all oppressed people.

Involvement in Women's Rights:

Matilda's involvement in the abolitionist movement naturally led her to become engaged in the women's rights movement. She recognized the parallels between the oppression of enslaved people and the subjugation of women, advocating for the rights of both groups with equal fervor.

Matilda co-authored "The History of Woman Suffrage" alongside Susan B. Anthony and Elizabeth Cady Stanton, documenting the history of the women's suffrage movement and the contributions of its leaders. She played a crucial role in organizing women's rights conventions and mobilizing support for women's suffrage, challenging societal norms and demanding equality under the law.

Legacy:

Matilda Joslyn Gage passed away on March 18, 1898, but her legacy lives on in the hearts and minds of activists and advocates for social justice. She is remembered as a fearless champion of women's rights and abolition, whose unwavering commitment to equality and justice continues to inspire generations of activists striving for a more just and equitable world.

Martha Coffin Wright

A Beacon of Hope on the Underground Railroad

Martha Coffin Wright, born on December 25, 1806, in Boston, Massachusetts, was a pioneering Quaker abolitionist and women's rights activist whose unwavering commitment to justice and equality left an indelible mark on the history of social reform in the United States. Through her courageous efforts on the Underground Railroad and her tireless advocacy for women's suffrage, she became a beacon of hope for enslaved people seeking freedom and for women striving for equality.

Early Life and Education:

Martha was born into a prominent Quaker family known for its commitment to social justice and reform. Her parents, Thomas and Anna Coffin, instilled in her a strong sense of moral responsibility and a deep compassion for the plight of the oppressed. Raised in an environment that valued education and enlightenment, Martha received a comprehensive education, which included instruction in literature, history, and philosophy.

Marriage and Family Life:

In 1824, at the age of eighteen, Martha married David Wright, a fellow Quaker and abolitionist. Their marriage was marked by mutual respect, shared values, and a deep commitment to social justice. Together, they raised seven children in a household that prioritized principles of equality, compassion, and activism.

Persecution and Opposition:

Martha's activism often brought her into conflict with the conservative forces of society, who sought to maintain the status quo and resist social change. She faced persecution and harassment from her detractors, who viewed her as a threat to their vested interests and sought to silence her voice.

Despite the risks, Martha remained steadfast in her commitment to justice and equality. She refused to be intimidated or deterred by the obstacles in her path, continuing to advocate for the rights and dignity of all people with unwavering courage and conviction.

Involvement in the Abolitionist Movement:

Martha's commitment to social justice led her to become actively involved in the abolitionist movement. Inspired by her Quaker faith and her family's legacy of activism, she joined the fight against slavery, advocating for its immediate and unconditional abolition.

As a key figure on the Underground Railroad, Martha played a crucial role in helping enslaved people escape to freedom. She provided shelter, food, and clothing to fugitive slaves, risking her own safety and freedom to assist those in need. Martha worked closely with other abolitionists, including her close friend Harriet Tubman, to coordinate escape routes and safe houses along the Underground Railroad.

Involvement in Women's Rights:

In addition to her work in the abolitionist movement, Martha was also a vocal advocate for women's rights and gender equality. She recognized the interconnectedness of the struggles for abolition and women's suffrage, advocating for the rights and dignity of all oppressed people.

Martha participated in women's rights conventions, where she spoke out against the injustices faced by women and called for legal and social reforms to ensure gender equality. She believed that women had a vital role to play in the fight for social justice and urged them to assert their rights and demand equal treatment under the law.

Legacy:

Martha Coffin Wright passed away on January 4, 1875, but her legacy lives on in the hearts and minds of activists and advocates for social justice. She is remembered as a fearless champion of abolition and women's rights, whose unwavering commitment to justice and equality continues to inspire generations of activists striving for a more just and equitable world.

Rebecca Buffum Spring

Eloquent and Passionate

Rebecca Buffum Spring, born on May 12, 1803, in Smithfield, Rhode Island, emerged as a steadfast advocate for abolition and women's rights in 19th-century America. As a devout Quaker, she was guided by principles of justice, equality, and compassion, dedicating her life to the pursuit of freedom and social reform. Through her activism in the Underground Railroad and her tireless advocacy for women's rights, Rebecca became a beacon of hope for the oppressed and marginalized.

Early Life and Education:

Rebecca Buffum was born into a Quaker family deeply committed to the principles of peace, equality, and social justice. Her parents, Arnold Buffum and Hannah White Buffum, instilled in her a strong sense of moral responsibility and a belief in the inherent dignity and worth of every human being. Growing up in a household that valued education and enlightenment, Rebecca received a comprehensive education, which included instruction in literature, history, and theology.

Marriage and Family Life:

In 1829, at the age of twenty-six, Rebecca married Dr. Samuel Spring, a fellow abolitionist and social reformer. Their marriage was marked by mutual respect, shared values, and a commitment to social justice. Together, they raised seven children in a household that prioritized compassion, empathy, and activism.

Persecution and Opposition:

Rebecca's activism often brought her into conflict with the conservative forces of society, who sought to maintain the status quo and resist social change. She faced persecution and harassment from her detractors, who viewed her as a threat to their vested interests and sought to silence her voice. Despite the opposition she faced, Rebecca remained steadfast in her commitment to justice and equality, refusing to be intimidated or deterred by the obstacles in her path.

Involvement in the Abolitionist Movement:

Rebecca's commitment to social justice led her to become actively involved in the abolitionist movement. Inspired by her Quaker faith and her belief in the inherent dignity of all human beings, she dedicated herself to the cause of ending slavery and promoting racial equality.

As a member of the Rhode Island Anti-Slavery Society, Rebecca participated in anti-slavery lectures, rallies, and protests, using her voice to amplify the calls for freedom and emancipation. She also played a key role in the Underground Railroad, providing shelter and support to escaped slaves fleeing to freedom.

Rebecca's activism extended beyond her local community, as she traveled throughout New England, speaking out against the evils of slavery and mobilizing support for the abolitionist cause. Her eloquent speeches and passionate advocacy helped to galvanize public opinion and build momentum for the anti-slavery movement.

Involvement in Women's Rights:

In addition to her work in the abolitionist movement, Rebecca was also a vocal advocate for women's rights and gender equality. She believed strongly in the need for women to have a voice in society and to be treated as equals.

Rebecca actively participated in women's rights conventions and meetings, where she advocated for women's suffrage, equal pay, and access to education and employment. She saw the struggle for women's rights as inseparable from the fight against slavery, recognizing the interconnectedness of all forms of oppression and injustice.

Legacy:

Rebecca Buffum Spring passed away on September 6, 1872, but her legacy lives on in the hearts and minds of activists and advocates for social justice. She is remembered as a fearless champion of abolition and women's rights, whose unwavering commitment to justice and equality continues to inspire generations of activists striving for a more just and equitable world.

Catharine Beecher

A Pioneer of Education and Social Reform

Catharine Esther Beecher, born on September 6, 1800, in East Hampton, New York, was a prominent American educator, writer, and social reformer. Throughout her life, she advocated for various social reforms, including the abolition of slavery and the advancement of women's education. Catharine's innovative ideas and tireless activism left a lasting impact on American society, shaping the landscape of education and social reform in the 19th century.

Early Life and Education:

Catharine was the eldest daughter of the famous minister Lyman Beecher and his wife, Roxana Foote Beecher. Growing up in a devoutly religious and intellectually stimulating household, Catharine was surrounded by discussions about theology, philosophy, and social reform from a young age. Her parents believed strongly in the importance of education for both boys and girls, instilling in Catharine a love of learning and a commitment to intellectual pursuits.

Despite limited formal education opportunities for women at the time, Catharine received a comprehensive education at home, studying subjects such as mathematics, science, literature, and theology under the guidance of her father and other tutors. She demonstrated a keen intellect and a voracious appetite for knowledge, laying the foundation for her future career as an educator and reformer.

Marriage and Family Life:

Catharine never married, choosing instead to dedicate her life to her work as an educator and social reformer. She remained close to her family throughout her life, particularly her siblings, many of whom were also involved in the fields of education and social reform. Catharine's close-knit family provided her with support and encouragement as she pursued her ambitious goals and sought to make a difference in the world.

Persecution and Opposition:

As a vocal advocate for social reform, Catharine faced opposition and criticism from conservative forces within American society. She encountered resistance from those who opposed her ideas about women's education and the abolition of slavery, who sought to maintain traditional gender roles and uphold the institution of slavery.

Despite the challenges she faced, Catharine remained steadfast in her convictions and continued to advocate for her beliefs with passion and determination. She refused to be silenced or deterred by the obstacles in her path, viewing opposition as a sign that she was challenging the status quo and making progress towards positive change.

Involvement in the Abolitionist Movement:

Catharine's commitment to social reform led her to become actively involved in the abolitionist movement. Inspired by her father's anti-slavery beliefs and the teachings of her brother, the renowned abolitionist Henry Ward Beecher, she joined the fight against slavery, advocating for its immediate and unconditional abolition.

Catharine used her platform as a writer and educator to raise awareness about the horrors of slavery and to mobilize support for the abolitionist cause. She penned articles, essays, and pamphlets that exposed the brutality of the slave system and called for its abolition. Catharine believed that education was key to ending slavery, arguing that by educating the public about the injustices of slavery, they would be inspired to take action to end it.

Involvement in Women's Education:

One of Catharine's most significant contributions to American society was her advocacy for women's education. She believed strongly that women should receive a quality education that would enable them to fulfill their potential and contribute meaningfully to society. Catharine argued that by educating women, society as a whole would benefit, as educated mothers would raise educated children who would become productive members of society.

To advance her vision of women's education, Catharine founded the Hartford Female Seminary in 1823, one of the first institutions in the United States dedicated to providing a rigorous academic education for women. The seminary offered a comprehensive curriculum that included subjects such as mathematics, science, literature, and history, preparing women for careers as teachers, writers, and social reformers.

Catharine also authored several influential books on women's education, including "A Treatise on Domestic Economy" and "The American Woman's Home," which outlined her ideas about the importance of education for women and provided practical advice for managing household affairs. Her writings helped to popularize the idea of women's education and inspired generations of women to pursue intellectual and professional pursuits.

Legacy:

Catharine Beecher passed away on May 12, 1878, but her legacy lives on in the countless individuals whose lives have been touched by her pioneering work in the fields of education and social reform. She is remembered as a trailblazer, a visionary, and a tireless advocate for justice and equality. Catharine's ideas and activism continue to inspire educators, activists, and reformers around the world, reminding us of the power of education to transform lives and create a more just and equitable society.

Frances Wright

A Trailblazer for Social Reform

Frances Wright, born on September 6, 1795, in Dundee, Scotland, was a remarkable figure of the 19th century, whose tireless advocacy for social reform left an indelible mark on American society. As a lecturer, writer, and social reformer, Wright dedicated her life to advocating for various causes, including the abolition of slavery, women's rights, and social equality. Her bold ideas and unwavering commitment to justice challenged the status quo and inspired generations of activists striving for a more just and equitable world.

Early Life and Education:

Frances Wright was born into a wealthy and progressive Scottish family, who encouraged her intellectual pursuits and social conscience from a young age. Her father, James Wright, was a successful merchant and political reformer, while her mother, Camilla Campbell, instilled in Frances a love of learning and a sense of compassion for the less fortunate.

Despite her privileged upbringing, Frances was deeply troubled by the injustices she witnessed in society, including the plight of the poor and the oppressed. She embarked on a journey of self-discovery and intellectual exploration, seeking to understand the root causes of social inequality and to find ways to address them.

Marriage and Family Life:

Frances Wright never married, choosing instead to devote her life to her work as a social reformer and activist. She remained independent and fiercely dedicated to her principles, refusing to conform to the traditional gender roles expected of women at the time.

Persecution and Opposition:

Frances Wright faced persecution and opposition throughout her life due to her outspoken advocacy for social reform. As a woman challenging the norms of her time, she encountered resistance from conservative forces within society who sought to maintain the status quo.

Despite the challenges she faced, Frances remained undeterred in her pursuit of justice and equality. She refused to be silenced or intimidated by her detractors, continuing to speak out against injustice with courage and conviction.

Involvement in the Abolitionist Movement:

Frances Wright was deeply committed to the abolition of slavery and dedicated much of her life to advocating for its abolition. Inspired by the ideals of the Enlightenment and the principles of equality and liberty, she believed passionately in the inherent dignity and worth of every human being, regardless of race or background.

In 1825, Frances traveled to the United States, where she became involved in the abolitionist movement. She was shocked and appalled by the horrors of slavery she witnessed firsthand, and she resolved to do everything in her power to bring about its end.

Frances used her platform as a writer and lecturer to raise awareness about the brutality of slavery and to mobilize support for the abolitionist cause. She penned numerous articles and essays condemning slavery as a moral and social evil, calling for its immediate abolition.

In 1826, Frances Wright embarked on a bold social experiment known as the Nashoba Commune, located near Memphis, Tennessee. The commune was founded on the principles of racial equality and cooperation, with the goal of providing education and training for newly emancipated slaves. Although the commune ultimately failed to achieve its objectives, it served as a powerful symbol of Frances's commitment to social reform and her willingness to challenge the prevailing attitudes of her time.

Involvement in Women's Rights:

Frances Wright was also a passionate advocate for women's rights and gender equality. She believed strongly in the need for women to have a voice in society and to be treated as equals in the eyes of the law.

Frances used her platform as a writer and lecturer to speak out against the injustices faced by women, including their lack of political rights and economic independence. She argued that women should have the same rights and opportunities as men, including the right to vote and participate fully in public life.

Legacy:

Frances Wright passed away on December 13, 1852, but her legacy lives on in the hearts and minds of activists and reformers around the world. She is remembered as a trailblazer, a visionary, and a tireless advocate for justice and equality. Frances Wright's bold ideas and courageous activism continue to inspire generations of activists striving for a more just and equitable world.

Mary White Ovington

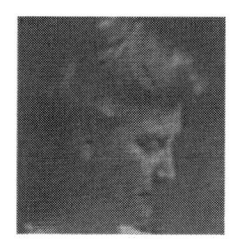

Co-founder of the NAACP

Mary White Ovington, born on April 11, 1865, in Brooklyn, New York, was a pioneering American suffragist and civil rights activist whose tireless advocacy for racial equality transformed the landscape of American society. As a co-founder of the NAACP (National Association for the Advancement of Colored People), Ovington played a pivotal role in the fight against racial discrimination and segregation. Her lifelong commitment to social justice and equality serves as a testament to the power of activism and perseverance in the face of injustice.

Early Life and Education:

Mary White Ovington was born into a prominent and socially conscious family in Brooklyn, New York. Her parents, Mary and Theodore Ovington, were staunch abolitionists and advocates for social reform, instilling in Mary a strong sense of social responsibility and a commitment to justice from a young age.

Growing up in a progressive household, Mary was exposed to discussions about race, inequality, and social justice from an early age. She attended Packer Collegiate Institute, a prestigious private school in Brooklyn, where she excelled academically and developed a passion for social reform.

After completing her education, Mary became increasingly involved in social activism, inspired by the example set by her parents and the values they instilled in her. She joined various reform organizations and devoted herself to fighting for the rights of the oppressed and marginalized.

Marriage and Family Life:

Mary White Ovington never married, choosing instead to dedicate her life to her work as an activist and advocate for social justice. She remained fiercely independent and committed to her principles, refusing to conform to the traditional gender roles expected of women at the time.

Persecution and Opposition:

As a vocal advocate for racial equality and civil rights, Mary White Ovington faced persecution and opposition from those who sought to maintain the status quo and uphold the system of racial segregation and discrimination. She encountered resistance from conservative forces within society who viewed her activism as a threat to their vested interests.

Despite the obstacles she faced, Mary remained undeterred in her pursuit of justice and equality. She refused to be intimidated or silenced by her detractors, continuing to speak out against racial injustice with courage and conviction.

Involvement in the Abolitionist Movement:

Mary White Ovington's commitment to racial equality was deeply rooted in her family's history of abolitionist activism. From a young age, she was inspired by the stories of her parents' involvement in the abolitionist movement and their efforts to fight against slavery and oppression.

As an adult, Mary became actively involved in the abolitionist movement, working alongside other activists to advocate for the abolition of slavery and the rights of African Americans. She participated in anti-slavery lectures, rallies, and protests, using her voice to amplify the calls for freedom and equality.

Involvement in Women's Suffrage:

In addition to her work in the abolitionist movement, Mary White Ovington was also a staunch advocate for women's suffrage and gender equality. She believed strongly in the need for women to have a voice in society and to be treated as equals in the eyes of the law.

Mary was actively involved in the women's suffrage movement, working alongside other suffragists to campaign for women's right to vote. She participated in suffrage marches, protests, and lobbying efforts, using her platform as an activist to advance the cause of women's rights.

Co-Founding the NAACP:

One of Mary White Ovington's most significant contributions to the fight for racial equality was her role in co-founding the NAACP in 1909. Inspired by the need for a national organization dedicated to combating racial discrimination and violence, Mary joined forces with other activists, including W.E.B. Du Bois and Ida B. Wells-Barnett, to establish the NAACP.

As one of the organization's founding members, Mary played a key role in shaping its mission and objectives, advocating for equal rights and opportunities for African Americans. She served on the NAACP's board of directors and played an active role in its day-to-day operations, helping to organize campaigns, events, and initiatives to advance the cause of civil rights.

Legacy:

Mary White Ovington passed away on July 15, 1951, but her legacy lives on in the countless individuals whose lives have been touched by her activism and advocacy. She is remembered as a trailblazer, a visionary, and a tireless champion for civil rights and racial justice. Mary White Ovington's commitment to equality and justice continues to inspire generations of activists and advocates fighting for a more inclusive and equitable society.

Caroline Weston

Keen intellect and a thirst for knowledge

Caroline Weston, born on May 3, 1808, in Wiscasset, Maine, was a dedicated abolitionist and women's rights activist whose tireless advocacy for social reform left a lasting impact on American society. Through her unwavering commitment to justice and equality, Weston played a crucial role in advancing the causes of abolitionism and women's rights during a pivotal period in American history. Her remarkable life and activism serve as a testament to the power of grassroots organizing and collective action in the fight for social justice.

Early Life and Education:

Caroline Weston was born into a middle-class family in Wiscasset, Maine, where she was raised with a strong sense of social responsibility and a commitment to community service. Her parents, Sarah and Isaac Weston, instilled in her the values of compassion, empathy, and justice from a young age, shaping her worldview and inspiring her to make a difference in the world.

Despite limited formal education opportunities for women at the time, Caroline demonstrated a keen intellect and a thirst for knowledge. She pursued her education through self-directed study, voraciously reading books and attending lectures on a wide range of subjects, including literature, history, and philosophy. Her passion for learning fueled her desire to contribute to the greater good and to fight against injustice wherever it existed.

Marriage and Family Life:

Caroline Weston never married, choosing instead to dedicate her life to her work as an activist and advocate for social reform. She remained fiercely independent and committed to her principles, refusing to conform to the traditional gender roles expected of women at the time.

Persecution and Opposition:

As a vocal advocate for abolitionism and women's rights, Caroline Weston faced persecution and opposition from those who sought to maintain the status quo and uphold the system of racial inequality and gender discrimination. She encountered resistance from conservative forces within society who viewed her activism as a threat to their vested interests.

Despite the challenges she faced, Caroline remained steadfast in her convictions and continued to speak out against injustice with courage and determination. She refused to be intimidated or silenced by her detractors, believing firmly in the righteousness of her cause and the power of collective action to bring about meaningful change.

Involvement in the Abolitionist Movement:

Caroline Weston's commitment to abolitionism was deeply rooted in her belief in the inherent dignity and equality of all people, regardless of race or background. Inspired by the teachings of the Quaker faith and the principles of human rights and social justice, she became actively involved in the abolitionist movement, working alongside other activists to advocate for the immediate and unconditional abolition of slavery.

As a member of the Boston Female Anti-Slavery Society, Caroline Weston played a crucial role in organizing lectures, rallies, and protests to raise awareness about the horrors of slavery and to mobilize support for the abolitionist cause. She used her platform as a writer and speaker to educate the public about the moral imperative of ending slavery and to challenge the prevailing attitudes of her time.

Involvement in Women's Rights:

In addition to her work in the abolitionist movement, Caroline Weston was also a passionate advocate for women's rights and gender equality. She believed strongly in the need for women to have a voice in society and to be treated as equals in the eyes of the law.

Caroline was actively involved in the women's rights movement, working alongside other suffragists to campaign for women's right to vote and to participate fully in public life. She participated in suffrage marches, protests, and lobbying efforts, using her platform as an activist to advance the cause of women's rights.

Friendships with Prominent Abolitionists:

Throughout her life, Caroline Weston forged close friendships with many prominent abolitionists, including William Lloyd Garrison, Lydia Maria

Child, and Wendell Phillips. These friendships were based on a shared commitment to justice and equality and a mutual desire to bring about meaningful social change.

Caroline collaborated with her abolitionist friends on various projects and initiatives, including the publication of abolitionist literature, the organization of anti-slavery lectures and rallies, and the support of fugitive slaves seeking refuge in the North. Together, they formed a tight-knit community of activists and advocates, united in their determination to end slavery and to build a more just and equitable society for all.

Legacy:

Caroline Weston passed away on December 5, 1882, but her legacy lives on in the countless individuals whose lives have been touched by her activism and advocacy. She is remembered as a trailblazer, a visionary, and a tireless champion for justice and equality. Caroline Weston's commitment to social reform continues to inspire generations of activists and advocates fighting for a more inclusive and equitable world.

Dorothea Dix

Champion of Social Reform and Humanitarian Advocate

Dorothea Dix, born on April 4, 1802, in Hampden, Maine, was a pioneering social reformer whose tireless advocacy transformed the landscape of mental health care and prison reform in the United States. Throughout her life, Dix dedicated herself to improving the lives of the marginalized and oppressed, working tirelessly to bring about meaningful change in the treatment of the mentally ill, prisoners, and African Americans. Her remarkable efforts paved the way for significant reforms in social welfare and established her as one of the most influential figures in American history.

Early Life and Education:

Dorothea Dix was born into a modest family in rural Maine, where she experienced poverty and hardship from a young age. Her father, Joseph Dix, was an itinerant preacher, and her mother, Mary Bigelow Dix, struggled to support the family financially. Despite the challenges she faced, Dorothea demonstrated an early aptitude for learning and a compassionate nature, qualities that would shape her future career as a social reformer.

At the age of twelve, Dorothea left home to live with her wealthy grandmother in Boston, Massachusetts, where she received a formal education and was exposed to the social injustices prevalent in society. Inspired by her grandmother's philanthropic work and her own observations of poverty and suffering, Dorothea developed a deep sense of empathy and a desire to make a difference in the world.

Marriage and Family Life:

Dorothea Dix never married, choosing instead to devote her life to her work as a social reformer and humanitarian advocate. She remained single throughout her life, maintaining her independence and focusing her energies on her activism and advocacy efforts.

Persecution and Opposition:

As a woman challenging the norms of her time and advocating for social reform, Dorothea Dix faced significant opposition and persecution from conservative forces within society. She encountered resistance from politicians, medical professionals, and religious leaders who were skeptical of her ideas and threatened by her calls for change.

Despite the obstacles she faced, Dorothea remained steadfast in her convictions and refused to be deterred by criticism or opposition. She continued to speak out against injustice with courage and determination, believing firmly in the righteousness of her cause and the importance of her work.

Advocacy for Mental Health Reform:

Dorothea Dix's advocacy for mental health reform was motivated by her personal experiences and observations of the deplorable conditions in which the mentally ill were often confined. In the early 19th century, individuals with mental illness were often housed in almshouses, jails, and asylums, where they were subjected to neglect, abuse, and inhumane treatment.

Dorothea embarked on a crusade to bring attention to the plight of the mentally ill and to advocate for their humane treatment and care. She conducted extensive research and investigations into the conditions of mental health facilities across the United States, documenting the abuses and injustices she uncovered and presenting her findings to state legislatures and Congress.

In 1843, Dorothea Dix presented a groundbreaking report to the Massachusetts legislature detailing the appalling conditions in which the mentally ill were housed and calling for the establishment of state-funded mental hospitals. Her efforts led to the passage of legislation authorizing the construction of the first public mental hospital in the United States, setting a precedent for mental health reform nationwide.

Over the course of her career, Dorothea Dix played a pivotal role in the establishment of dozens of mental hospitals and asylums across the

United States, revolutionizing the treatment of the mentally ill and championing the cause of mental health reform.

Advocacy for Prison Reform:

In addition to her work in the field of mental health reform, Dorothea Dix was also a passionate advocate for prison reform. She was deeply troubled by the inhumane conditions prevalent in prisons and jails, where inmates were subjected to overcrowding, unsanitary conditions, and brutal treatment.

Dorothea conducted extensive research into the conditions of prisons and jails across the United States, documenting the abuses and injustices she uncovered and calling for their reform. She lobbied state legislatures and Congress to enact laws and policies aimed at improving the treatment of prisoners and promoting rehabilitation and reintegration into society.

One of Dorothea Dix's most significant achievements in the field of prison reform was the establishment of the first federal penitentiary for women in the United States. In 1865, she successfully lobbied Congress to allocate funds for the construction of the Indiana Women's Prison, which served as a model for the humane treatment and rehabilitation of female inmates.

Advocacy for African Americans:

Throughout her career, Dorothea Dix was also an outspoken abolitionist who worked to improve conditions for African Americans. She was deeply troubled by the institution of slavery and the injustices suffered by African Americans, and she used her platform as a social reformer to advocate for their emancipation and equal rights.

During the Civil War, Dorothea Dix served as the Superintendent of Army Nurses for the Union Army, overseeing the recruitment and deployment of thousands of female nurses to military hospitals and field stations. She was deeply committed to providing compassionate care and support to wounded soldiers, regardless of their race or background, and she actively recruited African American women to serve as nurses in the Union Army.

Legacy:

Dorothea Dix passed away on July 17, 1887, but her legacy lives on in the countless individuals whose lives have been touched by her activism and advocacy. She is remembered as a trailblazer, a visionary, and a tireless champion for social reform and humanitarianism. Dorothea Dix's commitment to justice and equality continues to inspire generations of activists and advocates fighting for a more just and compassionate world.

Mary Townsend Seymour

A Trailblazer for Suffrage and Civil Rights

Mary Townsend Seymour, born on February 16, 1848, in Albany, New York, was a pioneering African American suffragist and civil rights activist whose remarkable life and tireless advocacy helped pave the way for social change and equality. From her early involvement in the abolitionist movement to her later efforts to secure voting rights for women and advance civil rights for African Americans, Mary Townsend Seymour's legacy remains an enduring testament to the power of perseverance and activism in the face of adversity.

Early Life and Education:

Mary Townsend Seymour was born into a free African American family in Albany, New York, during a time of great social upheaval and racial tension in the United States. Despite the challenges of growing up in a society marked by racism and discrimination, Mary's parents instilled in her a strong sense of pride in her African heritage and a belief in the importance of fighting for justice and equality.

From a young age, Mary showed a keen intellect and a passion for learning. She attended public schools in Albany, where she excelled academically and demonstrated a natural talent for leadership and public speaking. Her early experiences of witnessing racial injustice and inequality in her community fueled her desire to work towards a more just and equitable society.

Marriage and Family Life:

Mary Townsend Seymour married William Seymour, a fellow activist and community leader, in 1872. Together, they raised a family and shared a deep commitment to social justice and civil rights. William supported

Mary's activism and played an active role in the struggle for equality alongside her.

Persecution and Opposition:

As an African American woman advocating for social change in a deeply segregated and discriminatory society, Mary Townsend Seymour faced persecution and opposition at every turn. She encountered resistance from both white supremacists and patriarchal forces within the African American community who sought to maintain the status quo.

Despite the obstacles she faced, Mary remained undeterred in her pursuit of justice and equality. She refused to be silenced or intimidated by her detractors, drawing strength from her faith and her belief in the righteousness of her cause.

Involvement in the Abolitionist Movement:

Mary Townsend Seymour's activism began at an early age with her involvement in the abolitionist movement. Inspired by the teachings of Frederick Douglass, Sojourner Truth, and other prominent abolitionists, she became actively involved in efforts to end slavery and promote racial equality.

As a member of the Albany Anti-Slavery Society, Mary participated in lectures, rallies, and protests aimed at raising awareness about the horrors of slavery and mobilizing support for the abolitionist cause. She also worked tirelessly to support escaped slaves on the Underground Railroad, providing shelter, food, and assistance to those seeking freedom in the North.

Involvement in the Suffrage Movement:

After the abolition of slavery, Mary Townsend Seymour turned her attention to the fight for women's suffrage and civil rights. She recognized that true equality could only be achieved through the empowerment of women and the full participation of African Americans in the political process.

Mary became actively involved in the women's suffrage movement, working alongside other suffragists to advocate for the right of women to vote. She participated in suffrage marches, protests, and lobbying efforts, using her platform as an activist to advance the cause of women's rights.

In addition to her work for women's suffrage, Mary also fought for civil rights and social justice for African Americans. She campaigned against segregation and discrimination in all its forms, working to dismantle the systems of oppression that perpetuated racial inequality in American society.

Legacy:

Mary Townsend Seymour passed away on October 14, 1923, but her legacy lives on in the countless individuals whose lives have been touched by her activism and advocacy. She is remembered as a trailblazer, a visionary, and a tireless champion for suffrage and civil rights. Mary Townsend Seymour's commitment to social justice and equality continues to inspire generations of activists and advocates fighting for a more just and equitable world.

Clara Barton

Founder of the Red Cross

Clara Barton, born on December 25, 1821, in Oxford, Massachusetts, was a trailblazing nurse, humanitarian, and social reformer whose extraordinary life and work transformed the landscape of healthcare and philanthropy in the United States. Best known as the founder of the American Red Cross, Barton's legacy of compassion, courage, and activism continues to inspire generations of individuals committed to serving humanity and advancing social justice.

Early Life and Education:

Clara Barton was the youngest of five siblings born to Stephen Barton and Sarah Stone Barton. Raised in a household characterized by a strong sense of duty, compassion, and community service, Clara was deeply influenced by her parents' values and beliefs. Her father, a farmer and horse breeder, instilled in her a love for the outdoors and a spirit of independence, while her mother, a homemaker and devoutly religious woman, emphasized the importance of kindness, empathy, and charity.

Despite financial constraints, Clara's parents prioritized education and ensured that all their children received a solid foundation in reading, writing, and arithmetic. Clara demonstrated an early aptitude for learning and excelled academically, eagerly devouring books on a wide range of subjects and displaying a natural curiosity about the world around her.

Marriage and Family Life:

Clara Barton never married, choosing instead to devote her life to her work as a nurse and humanitarian. Throughout her life, she remained fiercely independent and committed to her principles, refusing to conform to the traditional gender roles expected of women at the time.

Persecution and Opposition:

As a woman working in the predominantly male-dominated fields of nursing and humanitarian aid, Clara Barton faced persecution and opposition from those who doubted her abilities and questioned her authority. She encountered resistance from conservative forces within society who viewed her activism as a threat to their entrenched power structures.

Despite the obstacles she faced, Clara remained undeterred in her pursuit of her goals, drawing strength from her unwavering belief in the righteousness of her cause and her deep commitment to serving others. She refused to be silenced or sidelined by her detractors, using her voice and her platform to advocate for those in need.

Involvement in the Abolitionist Movement:

Clara Barton's commitment to social justice and humanitarianism was deeply rooted in her upbringing and her personal values. Inspired by her parents' example of kindness, generosity, and compassion, she became actively involved in the abolitionist movement, working alongside other activists to advocate for the abolition of slavery and the rights of African Americans.

During the Civil War, Clara Barton volunteered as a nurse, providing medical care and aid to soldiers on the front lines. She witnessed firsthand the horrors of war and the suffering endured by those affected by conflict, further fueling her determination to alleviate human suffering and promote peace.

Involvement in the Suffrage Movement:

In addition to her work in the abolitionist movement, Clara Barton was also a vocal advocate for women's rights and gender equality. She recognized the importance of women having a voice in society and the need for them to be treated as equals in the eyes of the law.

Although Clara Barton's activism in the suffrage movement was less prominent than her work in nursing and humanitarian aid, she nonetheless supported the cause of women's rights and participated in suffrage events and rallies. She believed strongly in the need for women to have a seat at the table and to be involved in decision-making processes that affected their lives.

Founding of the American Red Cross:

Clara Barton's most enduring legacy is her role as the founder of the American Red Cross, a humanitarian organization dedicated to providing emergency assistance, disaster relief, and support to those in need. Inspired by her experiences as a nurse during the Civil War, Clara recognized the need for a permanent organization to coordinate relief efforts and provide aid to victims of natural disasters and other emergencies.

In 1881, Clara Barton established the American Red Cross, serving as its first president and guiding its growth and expansion over the next two decades. Under her leadership, the organization provided vital assistance to millions of people affected by disasters, including floods, fires, earthquakes, and epidemics, earning Clara Barton widespread recognition as the "Angel of the Battlefield" and the "Lady of the Lamp."

Legacy:

Clara Barton passed away on April 12, 1912, but her legacy lives on in the countless lives she touched and the enduring impact of her work. She is remembered as a pioneer, a humanitarian, and a trailblazer whose compassion, courage, and commitment to service continue to inspire people around the world. Clara Barton's tireless efforts to alleviate human suffering and promote social justice serve as a powerful reminder of the difference that one person can make in the world.

Lydia White Shattuck

A Champion for Justice and Equality

Lydia White Shattuck, born on June 6, 1822, in Concord, Massachusetts, was a pioneering American abolitionist and women's rights activist whose unwavering commitment to social justice and equality left an indelible mark on the history of reform movements in the United States. From her early involvement in the abolitionist cause to her later advocacy work for women's suffrage and civil rights, Lydia White Shattuck's life and legacy serve as a testament to the power of grassroots activism and collective action in the fight for a more just and equitable society.

Early Life and Education:

Lydia White was born into a Quaker family in Concord, Massachusetts, where she was raised with a deep commitment to the principles of peace, equality, and social justice. From a young age, Lydia demonstrated a keen intellect and a passion for learning, eagerly absorbing the teachings of her parents and community elders on the importance of standing up against injustice and oppression.

Despite limited educational opportunities for women at the time, Lydia's parents prioritized her education and ensured that she received a solid foundation in reading, writing, and arithmetic. Lydia's voracious appetite for knowledge led her to pursue self-directed study, delving into a wide range of subjects, including literature, history, and philosophy.

Marriage and Family Life:

In 1845, Lydia White married Samuel Shattuck, a fellow abolitionist and social reformer, with whom she shared a deep commitment to the cause of justice and equality. Together, they raised a family and worked tirelessly to advance the principles of abolitionism and women's rights.

Persecution and Opposition:

As outspoken advocates for social reform in a society marked by entrenched racism and sexism, Lydia White Shattuck and her husband faced persecution and opposition from those who sought to maintain the status quo and uphold systems of inequality and oppression. They encountered resistance from conservative forces within society who viewed their activism as a threat to their vested interests.

Despite the personal risks and challenges they faced, Lydia and Samuel remained steadfast in their convictions and continued to speak out against injustice with courage and determination. They refused to be intimidated or silenced by their detractors, believing firmly in the righteousness of their cause and the power of collective action to bring about meaningful change.

Involvement in the Abolitionist Movement:

Lydia White Shattuck's commitment to abolitionism was deeply rooted in her Quaker faith and her belief in the inherent dignity and equality of all people. Inspired by the teachings of Quaker abolitionists like William Lloyd Garrison and Lucretia Mott, Lydia became actively involved in the abolitionist movement, working alongside other activists to advocate for the immediate and unconditional abolition of slavery.

As a member of the Concord Female Anti-Slavery Society, Lydia played a crucial role in organizing lectures, rallies, and protests to raise awareness about the horrors of slavery and to mobilize support for the abolitionist cause. She used her platform as a writer and speaker to educate the public about the moral imperative of ending slavery and to challenge the prevailing attitudes of her time.

Involvement in the Women's Rights Movement:

In addition to her work in the abolitionist movement, Lydia White Shattuck was also a passionate advocate for women's rights and gender equality. She recognized that true liberation could only be achieved through the empowerment of women and the dismantling of patriarchal systems of oppression.

Lydia was actively involved in the women's rights movement, working alongside other suffragists to campaign for women's right to vote and to participate fully in public life. She participated in suffrage marches, protests, and lobbying efforts, using her platform as an activist to advance the cause of women's rights.

Legacy:

Lydia White Shattuck passed away on September 20, 1889, but her legacy lives on in the countless individuals whose lives have been touched by her activism and advocacy. She is remembered as a trailblazer, a visionary, and a tireless champion for justice and equality. Lydia White Shattuck's commitment to social reform continues to inspire generations of activists and advocates fighting for a more just and equitable world.

Anna Elizabeth Dickinson

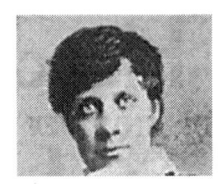

Impassioned Voice of Emancipation

Anna Elizabeth Dickinson, born on October 28, 1842, in Philadelphia, Pennsylvania, emerged as one of the most influential orators and activists of the 19th century, leaving an indelible mark on the history of the United States. A tireless advocate for abolition, women's rights, and civil rights, Dickinson's powerful speeches and unwavering commitment to social justice earned her widespread acclaim and admiration. From her early years as a precocious child prodigy to her later role as a prominent advocate for equality and reform, Anna Elizabeth Dickinson's life and legacy continue to inspire generations of activists and advocates striving for a more just and equitable society.

Early Life and Education:

Anna Elizabeth Dickinson was born into a Quaker family in Philadelphia, Pennsylvania, where she spent her formative years immersed in a culture of intellectual curiosity, social activism, and moral integrity. From a young age, Anna demonstrated an exceptional intellect and a natural gift for public speaking, captivating audiences with her eloquence and passion.

Despite financial hardships, Anna's parents prioritized her education and encouraged her intellectual pursuits, instilling in her a deep sense of social responsibility and a commitment to the principles of equality and justice. Anna's voracious appetite for knowledge led her to devour books on a wide range of subjects, from history and literature to politics and philosophy, laying the foundation for her future career as a renowned lecturer and activist.

Marriage and Family Life:

Anna Elizabeth Dickinson never married, choosing instead to dedicate her life to her work as an orator and advocate for social reform. While she valued companionship and friendship, Anna remained fiercely independent and committed to her principles, refusing to conform to the traditional gender roles expected of women at the time.

Persecution and Opposition:

As a woman speaking out on controversial issues such as abolition and women's rights in a society dominated by patriarchal norms and entrenched racism, Anna Elizabeth Dickinson faced persecution and opposition from those who sought to silence her and undermine her credibility. She encountered resistance from conservative forces within society who viewed her activism as a threat to their vested interests.

Despite the personal risks and challenges she faced, Anna remained undeterred in her pursuit of justice and equality, drawing strength from her convictions and her belief in the power of words to effect meaningful change. She refused to be intimidated or silenced by her detractors, using her voice and her platform to shine a light on the injustices of her time and to inspire others to join her in the fight for social justice.

Involvement in the Abolitionist Movement:

Anna Elizabeth Dickinson's commitment to abolitionism was deeply rooted in her Quaker upbringing and her belief in the inherent dignity and equality of all people. Inspired by the teachings of Quaker abolitionists such as Lucretia Mott and William Lloyd Garrison, Anna became actively involved in the abolitionist movement, speaking out against the evils of slavery and advocating for its immediate and unconditional abolition.

As a young woman, Anna gained national prominence for her impassioned speeches denouncing slavery and calling for its abolition. She traveled across the country, delivering powerful lectures that moved audiences to action and helped galvanize support for the abolitionist cause. Anna's eloquence and moral clarity made her a formidable advocate for freedom and equality, earning her the admiration of fellow abolitionists and the respect of her audiences.

Involvement in the Women's Rights Movement:

In addition to her work in the abolitionist movement, Anna Elizabeth Dickinson was also a passionate advocate for women's rights and gender equality. She recognized that true liberation could only be achieved through the empowerment of women and the dismantling of patriarchal systems of oppression.

Anna spoke out against the inequalities faced by women in American society, calling for equal rights and opportunities for women in all areas of life. She participated in women's rights conventions and rallies, lending her voice and her influence to the struggle for women's suffrage and other women's rights causes.

Participation in Women's Voting Rights Processes:

Anna Elizabeth Dickinson actively participated in the women's suffrage movement, advocating for the right of women to vote and to participate fully in the political process. She recognized that political empowerment was essential for women to achieve equality and to influence the laws and policies that affected their lives.

Anna spoke at suffrage rallies and meetings, urging women to demand their rights and to exercise their political power. She used her platform as a renowned lecturer to raise awareness about the importance of women's suffrage and to mobilize support for the cause.

Legacy:

Anna Elizabeth Dickinson passed away on October 22, 1932, but her legacy lives on in the countless individuals whose lives have been touched by her activism and advocacy. She is remembered as a trailblazer, a visionary, and a tireless champion for justice and equality. Anna Elizabeth Dickinson's powerful speeches and passionate activism continue to inspire generations of activists and advocates fighting for a more just and equitable world.

Sarah Margaret Fuller

Editor of The "Dial" A Voice for Social Reform and Women's Rights

Sarah Margaret Fuller, born on May 23, 1810, in Cambridgeport, Massachusetts, was a pioneering American journalist, critic, and women's rights advocate whose influential writings and strong activism helped shape the landscape of social reform in the United States during the 19th century. Best known for her work as an editor of the transcendentalist journal "The Dial" and her groundbreaking book "Woman in the Nineteenth Century," Fuller's legacy as a champion of equality and justice continues to inspire generations of activists and intellectuals.

Early Life and Education:

Sarah Margaret Fuller was the eldest child of Timothy Fuller, a prominent lawyer and politician, and Margaret Crane Fuller, a devoutly religious woman with a keen intellect and a strong sense of social responsibility. From an early age, Sarah displayed a precocious intellect and a voracious appetite for learning, devouring books on a wide range of subjects and demonstrating a talent for writing and critical thinking.

Despite the limited educational opportunities available to women in the early 19th century, Sarah received a thorough education at home under the guidance of her father, who believed strongly in the importance of intellectual development for both his sons and daughters. Under his tutelage, Sarah studied Latin, Greek, philosophy, and literature, laying the foundation for her later career as a writer and intellectual.

Marriage and Family Life:

In 1839, Sarah Margaret Fuller married Giovanni Angelo Ossoli, an Italian revolutionary and former Marquis, with whom she had a son, Angelo Eugene Philip Ossoli. The marriage was unconventional for its time, marked by intellectual partnership and mutual respect rather than traditional gender roles. Despite their ideological differences and the challenges of living in a society that frowned upon such unions, Sarah and Giovanni shared a deep love and commitment to their family and their shared ideals.

Persecution and Opposition:

As a woman engaged in public intellectual and political discourse in the male-dominated spheres of journalism and social reform, Sarah Margaret Fuller faced persecution and opposition from conservative forces within society who viewed her activism as a threat to the established order. She encountered resistance from those who sought to silence her voice and undermine her credibility, questioning her qualifications and disparaging her ideas.

Despite the obstacles she faced, Sarah remained undeterred in her pursuit of social justice and equality, drawing strength from her convictions and her belief in the power of knowledge and enlightenment to effect positive change. She refused to be silenced or marginalized by her detractors, using her platform as a writer and public speaker to advocate for the rights and dignity of women and marginalized communities.

Involvement in the Abolitionist Movement:

Sarah Margaret Fuller's commitment to social reform was deeply rooted in her belief in the inherent dignity and equality of all people, regardless of race or gender. Inspired by the ideals of the transcendentalist movement and the teachings of figures like Ralph Waldo Emerson and Margaret Fuller, she became actively involved in the abolitionist movement, working alongside other activists to advocate for the end of slavery and the rights of African Americans.

As the editor of "The Dial," a leading transcendentalist journal, Sarah used her platform to amplify the voices of abolitionists and to raise awareness about the moral imperative of ending slavery. She wrote extensively on the subject, condemning the institution of slavery as a moral outrage and calling for its immediate abolition.

Involvement in the Women's Rights Movement:

In addition to her work in the abolitionist movement, Sarah Margaret Fuller was also a passionate advocate for women's rights and gender equality. She recognized the need for women to have a voice in public life and the importance of challenging the patriarchal norms and structures that constrained their freedom and agency.

Sarah's groundbreaking book "Woman in the Nineteenth Century," published in 1845, is widely regarded as one of the foundational texts of the women's rights movement. In it, she argued for the full intellectual and spiritual equality of women, challenging prevailing notions of female inferiority and advocating for women's right to education, employment, and political participation.

Legacy:

Sarah Margaret Fuller's untimely death at the age of 40 in a shipwreck off the coast of Fire Island, New York, in 1850 cut short a life marked by intellectual brilliance and passionate advocacy for social reform. Yet, her legacy as a pioneering journalist, critic, and women's rights advocate continues to inspire generations of activists and intellectuals.

Through her writings and activism, Sarah Margaret Fuller helped to lay the groundwork for the women's rights movement and advance the cause of social justice and equality in the United States. Her commitment to challenging injustice and expanding the boundaries of freedom and opportunity for all people remains as relevant today as it was during her lifetime, a testament to the enduring power of her ideas and her vision for a more just and equitable society.

Lillie Devereux Blake

A Trailblazer for Women's Rights and Social Justice

Lillie Devereux Blake, born on August 12, 1833, in Raleigh, North Carolina, was a pioneering American suffragist, reformer, and advocate for women's rights and education. From her early involvement in the abolitionist movement to her later activism for women's suffrage and gender equality, Blake's tireless efforts to advance the cause of social justice continue to inspire generations of activists and advocates fighting for equality and empowerment.

Early Life and Education:

Lillie Devereux was born into a prominent Southern family with a long tradition of public service and intellectual achievement. Her father, William Devereux, was a respected lawyer and judge, while her mother, Elizabeth Stone Devereux, was a devoted homemaker and philanthropist. Growing up in a household marked by privilege and opportunity, Lillie received a thorough education at home, where she was encouraged to pursue her intellectual interests and develop her talents.

Despite the cultural norms and societal expectations that limited the educational opportunities available to women in the antebellum South, Lillie's parents were progressive thinkers who believed strongly in the importance of education for both their sons and daughters. They provided Lillie with access to a wide range of books and resources, fostering her love of learning and her commitment to social justice from an early age.

Marriage and Family Life:

In 1855, Lillie Devereux married Frank G. Blake, a lawyer and abolitionist from New York City, with whom she had two children, Katherine and Herman. The marriage brought Lillie into contact with the vibrant intellectual and cultural scene of New York City, where she would become actively involved in the abolitionist and women's rights movements.

Persecution and Opposition:

As a woman engaged in public advocacy and activism in the male-dominated spheres of politics and social reform, Lillie Devereux Blake faced persecution and opposition from conservative forces within society who viewed her activism as a threat to the established order. She encountered resistance from those who sought to maintain traditional gender roles and deny women access to political power and social equality.

Despite the challenges she faced, Lillie remained steadfast in her commitment to social justice and gender equality, using her voice and her platform to advocate for the rights and dignity of women and marginalized communities. She refused to be silenced or sidelined by her detractors, drawing strength from her convictions and her belief in the power of collective action to effect positive change.

Involvement in the Abolitionist Movement:

Lillie Devereux Blake's commitment to social justice was deeply rooted in her upbringing and her family's values. Inspired by her parents' example of compassion and service, she became actively involved in the abolitionist movement, working alongside other activists to advocate for the end of slavery and the rights of African Americans.

As a member of the New York Woman's Rights Committee, Lillie participated in lectures, rallies, and protests to raise awareness about the horrors of slavery and mobilize support for the abolitionist cause. She used her platform as a writer and speaker to condemn the institution of slavery as a moral outrage and to call for its immediate abolition.

Involvement in the Women's Suffrage Movement:

In addition to her work in the abolitionist movement, Lillie Devereux Blake was also a passionate advocate for women's suffrage and gender equality. She recognized the importance of women having a voice in public life and the need for them to be treated as equals in the eyes of the law.

As a founding member of the New York State Woman Suffrage Association, Lillie played a leading role in the fight for women's voting rights, organizing campaigns, lobbying legislators, and speaking out against the injustice of denying women the right to vote. She believed strongly in the need for women to have a seat at the table and to be involved in decision-making processes that affected their lives.

Legacy:

Lillie Devereux Blake passed away on December 30, 1913, but her legacy as a pioneering suffragist and advocate for women's rights and social justice lives on. She is remembered as a trailblazer, a visionary, and a tireless champion for equality and empowerment.

Through her activism and advocacy, Lillie Devereux Blake helped to lay the groundwork for the women's rights movement and advance the cause of social justice and equality in the United States. Her commitment to challenging injustice and expanding the boundaries of freedom and opportunity for all people remains as relevant today as it was during her lifetime, a testament to the enduring power of her ideas and her vision for a more just and equitable society.

Harriet Tubman

The Conductor of the Underground Railroad and Union Soldier

Introduction:

Harriet Tubman, born into slavery, emerged as one of the most courageous figures in American history, renowned for her role as a conductor on the Underground Railroad. Born Araminta Ross in Dorchester County, Maryland, around 1822, Tubman's life was marked by resilience, bravery, and an unwavering commitment to freedom. This essay will delve into the remarkable life of Harriet Tubman, exploring her early childhood, marriages, persecution, and her significant contributions to the abolitionist movement and women's rights.

Early Childhood:

Harriet Tubman was born into slavery on a plantation in Dorchester County, Maryland, around 1822. Born to enslaved parents, Harriet, then known as Araminta Ross, endured the harsh realities of slavery from a young age. Tubman experienced the cruelty of the institution firsthand, witnessing the separation of families, the brutality of overseers, and the constant threat of violence.

Despite the hardships she faced, Tubman demonstrated remarkable courage and resilience from an early age. As a child, she learned the skills of survival and navigation in the dense forests of Maryland, knowledge that would later prove invaluable in her efforts to lead enslaved individuals to freedom.

Marriages:

In 1844, Harriet Tubman married John Tubman, a free African American man. The marriage was short-lived, as Tubman's desire for freedom clashed with her husband's reluctance to escape. Although her marriage to John ended, Tubman's commitment to liberty only grew stronger.

In 1869, Harriet Tubman married again, this time to Nelson Davis, a veteran of the Union Army. The marriage lasted until Davis's death in 1888. Throughout her marriages, Tubman remained focused on her mission to liberate enslaved individuals and fight for the rights of African Americans.

Persecution and Escape:

Harriet Tubman's determination to secure her freedom led her to escape from slavery in 1849. Fearing that she would be sold and separated from her family, Tubman embarked on a perilous journey northward, relying on her instincts and her knowledge of the land to evade capture.

Tubman's escape marked the beginning of her remarkable career as a conductor on the Underground Railroad. Over the course of 11 years, Tubman made approximately 13 dangerous trips back to Maryland, leading more than 70 enslaved individuals, including family members and friends, to freedom in the northern states and Canada.

Persecuted by slaveholders and slave catchers who sought to capture and return her to bondage, Tubman lived under constant threat of discovery and capture. Despite the dangers she faced, Tubman remained undeterred, risking her lifetime and again to rescue others from the horrors of slavery.

Abolitionist Activism:

Harriet Tubman's work as a conductor on the Underground Railroad solidified her reputation as one of the most prominent figures in the abolitionist movement. Her daring rescues and fearless leadership earned her the nickname "Moses" among the enslaved community.

In addition to her work on the Underground Railroad, Tubman was actively involved in abolitionist activities and organizations. She worked alongside prominent abolitionists such as Frederick Douglass and William Lloyd Garrison, advocating for the immediate and unconditional emancipation of enslaved individuals.

Tubman's contributions to the abolitionist cause extended beyond her efforts to free enslaved individuals. During the Civil War, she served as a nurse, scout, and spy for the Union Army, providing invaluable assistance to the cause of freedom.

Women's Rights Advocacy:

While Harriet Tubman's primary focus was on the abolition of slavery, she also recognized the importance of women's rights and gender equality. Tubman was a staunch advocate for women's suffrage, believing that women should have the right to vote and participate fully in the democratic process.

Despite facing discrimination and marginalization as a woman of color, Tubman remained steadfast in her commitment to women's rights. She spoke out against the injustices faced by women and fought for their inclusion in the broader struggle for equality.

Legacy:

Harriet Tubman's legacy as a freedom fighter, abolitionist, and women's rights advocate continues to inspire generations of individuals around the world. Her bravery, compassion, and unwavering dedication to the cause of freedom serve as a reminder of the power of individuals to effect change and make a difference in the world.

Conclusion:

Harriet Tubman's life story is a testament to the indomitable spirit of the human soul and the enduring quest for freedom and equality. From her humble beginnings as an enslaved child in Maryland to her heroic efforts as a conductor on the Underground Railroad, Tubman's journey embodies the triumph of hope over despair and the resilience of the human spirit in the face of adversity. Her legacy will continue to inspire future generations to fight for justice, equality, and freedom for all.

Conclusion

My thoughts on the emergence of women as a force to demand freedom across the board is this. That Juneteenth as a stand-alone holiday without the addition of a similar day to celebrate the 19th Amendment to the constitution is rewarding us for less than half the job done of opening the door to equality in America. It leaves the same tone as the 4th of July did when the Dred Scott Decision was still the law of the land. That African Americans could never be included as citizens. Women were left standing on the outside looking in even after 1866 as far as the law was concerned.

For that reason I feel the need for a national celebration to honor the real emancipation of half of the citizenry . I also believe it fitting that it be combined with the existing Juneteenth celebrations.

I do not belittle the importance of removing the murderous monstrosity of slavery from our shores, but leaving inequity in the voting place behind only opens the door for it to return in some form or other.

For instance, spousal abuse was rampant across all races. During the peak period of the abolitionists, statistics on spousal abuse States are scarce due to the lack of systematic data collection and reporting during that time. Additionally, domestic violence was often considered a private matter, and victims were often discouraged from seeking help or reporting abuse.

However, historical accounts, court records, and literature from the period provide some insight into the prevalence of spousal abuse during that time. Women's rights activists and social reformers of the 19th century, such as Susan B. Anthony and Elizabeth Cady Stanton, often highlighted the issue of domestic violence in their writings and speeches, indicating that it was a significant problem affecting many women.

In addition, please note that societal attitudes toward domestic violence and the legal response to it were vastly different during the 19th century compared to today. Women had limited legal recourse and societal support if they experienced abuse, and there were few resources available to assist victims. As a result, many instances of spousal abuse likely went unreported and undocumented.

As an old comedian named Moms Mabley once said, "If the mule die, you are still a slave," which is another way of saying that a slave by any other name is still a slave.

I close this work with the listing of the order in which women were granted the vote in the United States and the Seneca Falls Declaration 1848. Both must know historical items, as important in some cases as the Bill of Rights, because in the enlightened country the bill sought the create, some things fell through the cracks.

Lois Denise Africa

When and where women gained the right to vote

*Hawaii and Alaska are not represented because the right was already in the constitution when they joined the union

1. **Wyoming:** Wyoming was the first state to grant women the right to vote on December 10, 1869, when it was still a territory. It continued this practice upon becoming a state on July 10, 1890.

2. **Colorado:** Colorado granted women the right to vote on November 7, 1893.

3. **Utah:** Utah granted women the right to vote on February 12, 1870, but this right was revoked in 1887. It was later restored on February 12, 1895.

4. **Idaho:** Idaho granted women the right to vote on November 3, 1896.

5. **Washington:** Washington granted women the right to vote on November 8, 1910.

6. **California:** California granted women the right to vote on October 10, 1911.

7. **Arizona:** Arizona granted women the right to vote on November 5, 1912.

8. **Kansas:** Kansas granted women the right to vote in municipal elections in 1887 and in all elections on November 5, 1912.

9. **Oregon:** Oregon granted women the right to vote on November 5, 1912.

10. **Alaska:** Alaska granted women the right to vote on April 24, 1913.

11. **Illinois:** Illinois granted women presidential suffrage on June 26, 1913, and full suffrage on June 26, 1919.

12. **Montana:** Montana granted women the right to vote on November 3, 1914.

13. **Nevada:** Nevada granted women the right to vote on November 3, 1914.

14. **New York:** New York granted women the right to vote on November 6, 1917.

15. **Michigan:** Michigan granted women the right to vote on November 5, 1918.

16. **Oklahoma:** Oklahoma granted women the right to vote on November 5, 1918.

17. **South Dakota:** South Dakota granted women the right to vote on November 5, 1918.

18. **Texas:** Texas granted women presidential suffrage on June 28, 1919, and full suffrage on June 24, 1919.

19. **Nebraska:** Nebraska granted women the right to vote on November 10, 1919.

20. **Missouri:** Missouri granted women the right to vote on November 3, 1920.

21. **Arkansas:** Arkansas granted women the right to vote on November 3, 1920.

22. **Maine:** Maine granted women the right to vote on November 5, 1919.

23. **Louisiana:** Louisiana granted women the right to vote on June 18, 1920.

24. **North Dakota:** North Dakota granted women the right to vote on November 3, 1919.

25. **Ohio:** Ohio granted women the right to vote on November 7, 1917.

26. **Indiana:** Indiana granted women the right to vote on January 16, 1920.

27. **West Virginia:** West Virginia granted women the right to vote on March 10, 1920.

28. **New Hampshire:** New Hampshire granted women the right to vote on September 2, 1919.

29. **Colorado:** Colorado granted women the right to vote on November 7, 1893.

30. **Delaware:** Delaware granted women the right to vote on March 6, 1923.

31. **Minnesota:** Minnesota granted women the right to vote on September 8, 1919.

32. **Connecticut:** Connecticut granted women the right to vote on September 14, 1920.

33. **Massachusetts:** Massachusetts granted women the right to vote on November 5, 1918.

34. **Iowa:** Iowa granted women the right to vote on July 2, 1919.

35. **Wisconsin:** Wisconsin granted women the right to vote on June 10, 1919.

36. **Rhode Island:** Rhode Island granted women the right to vote on January 6, 1920.

37. **New Jersey:** New Jersey granted women the right to vote on February 9, 1920.

38. **Vermont:** Vermont granted women the right to vote on November 2, 1920.

39. **North Carolina:** North Carolina granted women the right to vote on August 18, 1920.

40. **South Carolina:** South Carolina granted women the right to vote on December 4, 1920.

41. **Georgia:** Georgia granted women the right to vote on December 20, 1920.

42. **Virginia:** Virginia granted women the right to vote on February 21, 1920.

43. **Florida:** Florida granted women the right to vote on May 26, 1920.

44. **Alabama:** Alabama granted women the right to vote on September 8, 1920.

45. **Kentucky:** Kentucky granted women the right to vote on January 6, 1920.

46. **Mississippi:** Mississippi granted women the right to vote on September 10, 1920.

47. **Tennessee:** Tennessee granted women the right to vote on August 18, 1920.

48. **Maryland:** Maryland granted women the right to vote on November 2, 1920.

The Seneca Falls Declaration 1848

Elizabeth Cady Stanton

1. Declaration of Sentiments

When, in the course of human events, it becomes necessary for one portion of the family of man to assume among the people of the earth a position different from that which they have hitherto occupied, but one to which the laws of nature and of nature's God entitle them, a decent respect to the opinions of mankind requires that they should declare the causes that impel them to such a course.

We hold these truths to be self-evident: that all men and women are created equal; that they are endowed by their Creator with certain inalienable rights; that among these are life, liberty, and the pursuit of happiness; that to secure these rights governments are instituted, deriving their just powers from the consent of the governed. Whenever any form of government becomes destructive of these ends, it is the right of those who suffer from it to refuse allegiance to it, and to insist upon the institution of a new government, laying its foundation on such principles, and organizing its powers in such form, as to them shall seem most likely to effect their safety and happiness. Prudence, indeed, will dictate that governments long established should not be changed for light and transient causes; and accordingly all experience hath shown that mankind are more disposed to suffer. while evils are sufferable, than to right themselves by abolishing the forms to which they are accustomed. But when a long train of abuses and usurpations, pursuing invariably the same object, evinces a design to reduce them under absolute despotism, it is their duty to throw off such government, and to provide new guards for their future security. Such has been the patient sufferance of the women under this government, and such is now the necessity which constrains them to demand the equal station to which they are entitled. The history of mankind is a history of repeated injuries and usurpations on the part of man toward woman, having in direct object the establishment of an absolute tyranny over her. To prove this, let facts be submitted to a candid world.

He has never permitted her to exercise her inalienable right to the elective franchise.

He has compelled her to submit to laws, in the formation of which she had no voice.

He has withheld from her rights which are given to the most ignorant and degraded men both natives and foreigners.

Having deprived her of this first right of a citizen, the elective franchise, thereby leaving her without representation in the halls of legislation, he has oppressed her on all sides.

He has made her, if married, in the eye of the law, civilly dead. He has taken from her all right in property. even to the wages she earns.

He has made her, morally. an irresponsible being. as she can commit many crimes with impunity, provided they be done in the presence of her husband.

In the covenant of marriage, she is compelled to promise obedience to her husband, he becoming, to all intents and purposes, her master, the law giving him power to deprive her of her liberty. and to administer chastisement.

He has so framed the laws of divorce, as to what shall be the proper causes, and in case of separation, to whom the guardianship of the children shall be given, as to be wholly regardless of the happiness of women, the law, in all cases, going upon a false supposition of the supremacy of man, and giving all power into his hands.

After depriving her of all rights as a married woman, if single, and the owner of property, he has taxed her to support a government which recognizes her only when her property can be made profitable to it.

He has monopolized nearly all the profitable employments, and from those she is permitted to follow, she receives but a scanty remuneration. He closes against her all the avenues to wealth and distinction which he considers most honorable to himself. As a teacher of theology, medicine, or law, she is not known.

He has denied her the facilities for obtaining a thorough education, all colleges being closed against her.

He allows her in Church, as well as State, but a subordinate position, claiming Apostolic authority for her exclusion from the ministry, and, with some exceptions, from any public participation in the affairs of the Church.

He has created a false public sentiment by giving to the world a different code of morals for men and women, by which moral delinquencies which exclude women from society, are not only tolerated, but deemed of little account in man.

He has usurped the prerogative of Jehovah himself, claiming it as his right to assign for her a sphere of action, when that belongs to her conscience and to her God.

He has endeavored, in every way that he could, to destroy her confidence in her own powers, to lessen her self-respect and to make her willing to lead a dependent and abject life.

Now, in view of this entire disfranchisement of one-half the people of this country, their social and religious degradation, in view of the unjust laws above mentioned, and because women do feel themselves aggrieved, oppressed, and fraudulently deprived of their most sacred rights, we insist that they have immediate admission to all the rights and privileges which belong to them as citizens of the United States.

In entering upon the great work before us, we anticipate no small amount of misconception, misrepresentation, and ridicule; but we shall use every instrumentality within our power to effect our object. We shall employ agents, circulate tracts, petition the State and National legislatures, and endeavor to enlist the pulpit and the press in our behalf. We hope this Convention will be followed by a series of Conventions embracing every part of the country.

2. resolutions

WHEREAS, The great precept of nature is conceded to be, that "man shall pursue his own true and substantial happiness." Blackstone in his Commentaries remarks, that this law of Nature being coeval with mankind, and dictated by God himself, is of course superior in obligation to any other. It is binding over all the globe, in all countries and at all times; no human laws are of any validity if contrary to this. and such of them as are valid, derive all their force. and all their validity, and all their authority, mediately and immediately, from this original; therefore,

Resolved,

That such laws as conflict, in any way with the true and substantial happiness of woman, are contrary to the great precept of nature and of no validity, for this is "superior in obligation to any other."

Resolved,

That all laws which prevent woman from occupying such a station in society as her conscience shall dictate, or which place her in a position inferior to that of man, are contrary to the great precept of nature, and therefore of no force or authority.

Resolved,

That woman is man's equal, was intended to be so by the Creator, and the highest good of the race demands that she should be recognized as such.

Resolved,

That the women of this country ought to be enlightened in regard to the laws under which they live, that they may no longer publish their degradation by declaring themselves satisfied with their present position, nor their ignorance, by asserting that they have all the rights they want.

Resolved.

That inasmuch as man, while claiming for himself intellectual superiority, does accord to woman moral superiority. it is pre-eminently his duty to encourage her to speak and teach. as she has an opportunity, in all religious assemblies.

Resolved,

That the same amount of virtue, delicacy, and refinement of behavior that is required of woman in the social state, should also be required of man, and the same transgressions should be visited with equal severity on both man and woman.

Resolved,

That the objection of indelicacy and impropriety, which is so often brought against woman when she addresses a public audience, comes with a very ill-grace from those who encourage, by their attendance, her appearance on the stage, in the concert. Or in feats of the circus.

Resolved,

That woman has too long rested satisfied in the circumscribed limits which corrupt customs and a perverted application of the Scriptures have marked out for her, and that it is time she should move in the enlarged sphere which her great Creator has assigned her.

Resolved,

That it is the duty of the women of this country to secure to themselves their sacred right to the elective franchise.

Resolved,

That the equality of human rights results necessarily from the fact of the identity of the race in capabilities and responsibilities.

Resolved, therefore.

That, being invested by the creator with the same capabilities, and the same consciousness of responsibility for their exercise, it is demonstrably the right and duty of woman, equally with man, to promote every righteous cause by every righteous means; and especially in regard to the great subjects of morals and religion, it is self-evidently her right to participate with her brother in teaching them, both in private and in public, by writing and by speaking. by any instrumentalities proper to be used. and in any assemblies proper to be held; and this being a self-evident truth growing out of the divinely implanted principles of human nature, any custom or authority adverse to it, whether modern or wearing the hoary sanction of antiquity, is to be regarded as a self- evident falsehood, and at war with mankind.

Resolved,

That the speedy success of our cause depends upon the zealous and untiring efforts of both men and women, for the overthrow of the monopoly of the pulpit. and for the securing to women an equal participation with men in the various trades. professions. and commerce.

Birthdates

1. Sarah Grimké: November 26, 1792

2. Angelina Grimké: February 20, 1805

3. Lucretia Mott: January 3, 1793

4. Elizabeth Cady Stanton: November 12, 1815

5. Lucy Stone: August 13, 1818

6. Susan B. Anthony: February 15, 1820

7. Sarah Parker Remond: June 6, 1826

8. Lydia Maria Child: February 11, 1802

9. Harriet Beecher Stowe: June 14, 1811

10. Sarah Moore Grimké: November 26, 1792

11. Abby Kelley Foster: January 15, 1811

12. Amelia Bloomer: May 27, 1818

13. Julia Ward Howe: May 27, 1819

14. Angelina Grimké Weld: February 20, 1805

15. Caroline Weston: January 6, 1808

16. Dorothea Dix: April 4, 1802

17. Antoinette Brown Blackwell: May 20, 1825

18. Maria Weston Chapman: July 25, 1806

19. Sarah Josepha Hale: October 24, 1788

20. Mary Livermore: December 19, 1820

21. Susan Paul: May 6, 1805

22. Ellen Craft: 1826 (exact date unknown)

23. Emily Howland: November 30, 1827

24. Hannah More: February 2, 1745

25. Anne Knight: November 2, 1786

26. Elizabeth Heyrick: December 4, 1769

27. Mary Prince: c. 1788 (exact date unknown)

28. Sarah Pugh: May 3, 1800

29. Caroline Chesebro': October 21, 1825

30. Mary Ann McCracken: July 8, 1770

31. Jane Grey Swisshelm: December 6, 1815

32. Matilda Joslyn Gage: March 24, 1826

33. Martha Coffin Wright: December 25, 1806

34. Rebecca Buffum Spring: June 24, 1803

35. Catharine Beecher: September 6, 1800

36. Frances Wright: September 6, 1795

37. Mary White Ovington: April 11, 1865

38. Caroline Weston: November 23, 1808

39. Dorothea Dix: April 4, 1802

40. Mary Townsend Seymour: March 9, 1848